Issues of Educational Leadership

Issues of Educational Leadership: Crisis Management during Challenging Times

Edited by Fern Aefsky

ROWMAN & LITTLEFIELD
London • New York

Published by Rowman & Littlefield
An imprint of The Rowman & Littlefield Publishing Group, Inc.
4501 Forbes Boulevard, Suite 200, Lanham, Maryland 20706
www.rowman.com

6 Tinworth Street, London SE11 5AL, United Kingdom

Copyright © 2021 by Fern Aefsky

All rights reserved. No part of this book may be reproduced in any form or by any electronic or mechanical means, including information storage and retrieval systems, without written permission from the publisher, except by a reviewer who may quote passages in a review.

British Library Cataloguing in Publication Information Available

Library of Congress Cataloging-in-Publication Data

Library of Congress Control Number: 2021933412

ISBN: 978-1-4758-5931-7 (cloth : alk. paper)
ISBN: 978-1-4758-5932-4 (pbk. : alk. paper)
ISBN: 978-1-4758-5933-1 (electronic)

♾️ The paper used in this publication meets the minimum requirements of American National Standard for Information Sciences—Permanence of Paper for Printed Library Materials, ANSI/NISO Z39.48-1992.

This book is dedicated to those teachers, administrators, and staff members who ensured that students' and stakeholders' needs were successfully met during challenging times of COVID-19, school shootings, and other crises.

Contents

Acknowledgment		ix
Introduction *Fern Aefsky*		1
1	Crisis Leadership *Fern Aefsky*	5
2	Crisis Management in a Pandemic: Voices from the Field *Renee Sedlack*	21
3	Leadership Supporting Teachers, Students, and Families during Crises *Melinda Carver*	35
4	Remote Learning: Lessons in Social Awareness and Transformative Action *Keya Mukherjee*	51
5	Crisis Leadership: Educating Students with Disabilities in Times of Change *Georgina Rivera-Singletary & Michael Bailey*	67
6	Mental Health Implications for Administrators, Faculty, Students, and Families *Susan Kinsella*	85
7	Crisis Management: Operational Challenges for Educational Leaders *Jodi Lamb, Ed Dadez, & Fern Aefsky*	101

8	Crisis Leadership: Lessons Learned *Fern Aefsky*	121

About the Contributors   129

About the Editor   133

Acknowledgment

Thank you to colleagues at Saint Leo University and practitioners and parents in various states for their collaboration and contributions. Much appreciated.

Introduction

Fern Aefsky

"Leadership and learning are indispensable to each other."
—President John F. Kennedy

Educational leaders must be prepared to lead during crisis. Leadership has been challenged with multiple crisis in recent years, including issues of school safety, school shootings, and medical crises such as SARs, H1N1, and the coronavirus (COVID-19). While each of these situations has resulted in multiple plans of actions, none has impacted our society as the current pandemic (COVID-19) has in terms of immediacy of needs and actions.

School and district leaders are in charge of managing many stakeholders, circumstances, and have the authority and responsibility to lead with ethical behavior (Al Halbusi et al., 2018). Integrity, resilience, and fairness help guide the components of ethical leadership that leaders need to model, communicate, and use as a framework for implementing and sustaining change in organizations (Hegarty & Moccia, 2018).

This book is targeted for aspiring leaders, leaders of educational systems, school buildings, and leaders of organizations that are connected in some way to educational systems and schools at all levels. The educational issues raised by the COVID pandemic began in March 2020. The leadership needs identified throughout this crisis exemplify many of the issues of crisis management that are applicable to other issues, such as school violence, school safety, social justice, accidents, and deaths, that occur in every district.

The overall status of quickly changing regulations, rules, and practices for educators resulted in multiple challenges during the pandemic crisis caused by COVID-19. Many issues impacted PK-12 schools and universities and leaders needed to act and develop immediate, short-term, and long-term plans, causing stress, challenges, and calls for action. These actions required changes in policies and government regulations at the federal, state, and local levels.

University presidents, school administrators, teachers, and staff members needed to change practice. School closings due to stay at home orders caused a domino effect with many other issues, such as childcare, parents losing jobs or working from home, figuring out how to get meals to students, and supplying students with needed technology. Other issues, such as increased domestic abuse and implementing social distancing while online learning occurs, with some having minimal support at home, have challenged many families.

School systems not only had to deal with specific academic needs of students and teachers learning how to work remotely and provide online instruction but also had to deal with pragmatics of students not coming to school, mental health and safety issues, and related support that children typically received in schools.

Many districts have many children who receive free or reduced-price lunch and breakfast; community partnerships support school programs financially, and many of the partners were closed temporarily or permanently due to required containment rules. Student and teacher morale suffered (Kurtz, April 2020). Not only did school personnel have to reinvent their professional job responsibilities, but many had the same home challenges facing most of society as well.

As the pandemic evolved, many things for educators changed on a daily basis. Trying to meet the needs of all students, staff, and faculty; planning for the reopening of schools; and state and federal changes in rules, regulations, and resources resulted in multiple events, challenges, and changes. Leaders had to collect changing data, make quick decisions, and implement the changes.

In the chapters of this book, details on these issues will be discussed at greater length, providing information to and for educators from the voices of practitioners. Collaborating was never more important, as daily and weekly changes related to the pandemic in each state changed what school personnel needed to do to keep systems in place to educate all children effectively.

While these issues were primary concerns of educators, parents, and politicians and bureaucrats who govern and manage schools, all typical issues of schools still remained entities that had to be dealt with effectively by leaders. Hiring of new faculty and staff members, scheduling, curriculum updates and changes, technology, assessments, and operational issues of financial implications, including but not limited to busing, food service, school safety, community partnerships, and state regulations implementation, all still existed and were part of the requirements as schools reopened.

The death of George Floyd on May 25, 2020, resulted in a call for issues of racism to be prioritized, as the Black Lives Matter movement, protests for justice, and a nationwide call for action occurred. Impact on schools and concerns of educators included how to deal with these issues with students, staff, and faculty upon schools reopening. Specific concerns shared by administrators included how to deal with those students who spent many months at home due to the pandemic, some of whom lived in family situations that may have discussed a lack of acceptance of people of different races, religions, and other beliefs. Typically, those students had positive experiences with friends who may belong to a category that their parent or family member talked negatively about and had daily contact with others who could discuss options. With the isolation caused by COVID-19, these were exacerbated and were something for educators to deal with upon students' return to the physical classroom.

In many districts across the country, families were asked what type of schooling they would be likely to want for their children: virtual, blended, or back on campus full time. This occurred in all levels of PK-20 education. This data enabled schools and universities to plan appropriately. However, staff and faculty were asked the same question and results did not align. School administrators had to manage three different scenarios at the same time, with less resources available.

Throughout the book, voices of students, families, and educators from multiple states shared their experiences, successes, and concerns. Hearing from stakeholders in the field from across the country enables us to inform practice wisely. Listening is key.

Readers of this book will be provided with multiple options and examples of how parents, educators, students, and administrators provided support and identified needs that needed to be addressed. Due to the rapidly changing situations that varied by state, we learned from one another's successes and challenges.

While the pandemic events drove much of the work of school and university leaders, the variables identified as a result of COVID-19 pandemic impacted educational leaders and their success in managing during a crisis, developing strategies and plans for organizational change, and allowing all stakeholders to be part of developing new policies and practices that make sense for all students, staff, and faculty.

REFERENCES

Al Halbusi, H., Ismail, M., & Omar, S. (May 2019). Examining the impact of ethical leadership on employees ethical behavior. *Journal of Technology Management and Business*, *6*(2), 389–48.

Hegarty, N., & Moccia, S. (2018). Components of ethical leadership and their importance in sustaining organizations over the long term. *Journal of Values-Based Leadership*, *11*(1), 1–10.

Kurtz, H. (April 10, 2020). National Survey Impact of Corona Virus on Schools: 10 Key Findings. *Education Week*. https://www.edweek.org/teaching-learning/national-survey-tracks-impact-of-coronavirus-on-schools-10-key-findings/2020/04.

Chapter 1

Crisis Leadership

Fern Aefsky

Educational leaders deal with many crises that impact local, state, national, and global issues. Crisis management is often a task of school building and district leadership teams. Hurricanes, bomb threats, tragic accidents, deaths of students and adults due to health issues, child abuse, and major discipline issues, to name a few.

As a result of the collaborative work done between stakeholders in communities and nationally, P-20 educational leaders have experience in developing and implementing plans regarding issues of school safety (Aefsky, 2019). However, nothing truly prepared leaders for the events that began in early 2020.

In January and February of 2020, schools and universities had wrapped up the first semester of studies with students and were starting the second semester, typical of each school year. The holidays were over, and in PK-12 schools across the country, focus was on curriculum achievement and spring assessments to measure growth and progress of student learning. Many students who were completing high school were looking forward to senior activities, such as proms, scholarship award events, and graduation activities.

At the university level, students were focused on completing second-semester courses and some students were preparing for meeting graduation requirements from bachelor's, master's, and doctoral levels. Typical campus activities, social and academic, were ongoing and planned.

Our world changed in the middle of March 2020, when COVID-19 became known nationwide, and the pandemic crisis stopped many things in the United States and globally. While politicians disagreed on how this happened, all of society was thrust into a situation that continually changed.

Government leaders focused initially on the medical crisis, where there were not enough supplies to keep healthcare workers safe from harm, not enough ICU beds to support needs of people in some states, and there were multiple issues between states in the Northeast and the federal government to quickly remediate and help people who came down with the virus. The number of cases continued to grow in states in the Northeast, where New York was the epicenter and much was done to try to contain the virus' spread.

The World Health Organization announced on March 11, 2020, that the COVID-19 was a global pandemic. As a result, over 421 million children and educational programs had been disrupted by school closures in multiple countries. Information was provided for prevention and control in schools (Bender, March 2020). In the document published by UNICEF, New York declared a public health emergency. As a result, there was a focus on protecting children and educational facilities.

Schools across the world were closed; recommendations were made for containing the virus, based on facts known at that time. Use of hand sanitizer, frequently washing hands, social distancing, collaborating with local health officials, following government rules and guidelines, and plan for continuity of learning all went into effect. In March, masks were not part of the discussion. By April, masks were recommended for all, with varying recommendations from federal and state government officials, confusing many.

School leaders needed to act quickly and without sound guidance or an established plan of action. Change occurred continuously, and scientists shared data that politicians in some states and nationally did not agree with, as questions arose continuously.

Schools closed and moved quickly to virtual learning environments, at both the PK-12 and university levels. Challenges occurred at public schools throughout the country as many educators had to create online learning opportunities for all students within a week to two weeks. There was a rush to train teachers, administrators, and students, resulting in recognition of a lack of technology for all students, lack of Internet, and lack of materials for teachers, parents, and students.

Companies and business partners assisted with immediate needs for hardware and Internet access. However, some families had four children and were loaned one laptop computer. Others had technology provided but did not know how to access information from home and did not have anyone who was able to guide them.

The disconnect between intent and reality was a significant challenge for all. People were told to shelter in place, and those lucky enough to keep jobs worked from home; others lost their jobs. The impact affected schools and communities, disrupted lives, and the economy for all.

The unemployment rate hit record numbers, and over 41 million people filed for unemployment benefits in a five-week time frame in the United States. People who had jobs had pay and benefits cut. While some government programs were put in place to assist, there was a marked delay in filing for benefits and receiving benefits for some.

The stressors for administrators, teachers, staff members, and families were monumental, and while these situations were evolving, parents were told they were responsible for ensuring that their students kept up with virtual education. The challenges for leaders in education exemplified the need for preparation for leading through crisis.

This book will present many aspects of crisis management and leadership by hearing from practitioners in the field. The impact of the pandemic is long term, and the United States is in the sixth month of a projected three-year minimum of impact for schools and educational systems. While school leaders dealt with the issues of the pandemic, which included financial, social-emotional, physical, and educational impacts, the other areas of managing and leading schools still existed and needed to be dealt with on behalf of students and the school community.

Information presented throughout this chapter was gathered from various stakeholders in schools across the country, sharing their reality as a parent, teacher, student, or administrator. These stories were important as educational leaders dealt with the pandemic crisis. Lessons learned from these experiences set the stage for other areas of crisis management. Each respondent was asked a few guiding questions in the areas of change, communication, and practice.

While policies and politics in states often guided plans, this book's focus is on how educators met the needs of students, faculty and staff, families, and communities as an example of leading through crises. Firsthand information from various stakeholders in multiple states identified many strategies for educators leading through any crises.

ADMINISTRATORS

E. E.—District Administrator, NY

Parents, faculty, and students became increasingly fearful of the unknown. March 12, 2020, was the last day student and faculty members attended school.

During the next week, the director of technology went to every school and collected all available laptops. The district had a 1:1 initiative for secondary students. The plan was to find computers for all children grades K-5.

Communication

A message was sent to all families in the district explaining our preparations for the long-term closure. The following is an excerpt of the communications sent to parents about virtual learning:

> As we all venture into this new way of doing "school" for a while, we wanted to share with you some guidance on what you can expect in the coming days and weeks. We recognize that an extended closure is a difficult time for all and we expect that you may still have some questions and concerns. We will remain in communication and keep you updated regularly.

Goal: Our goal during those next few weeks was to maintain continuity of students' educational experience. We knew that remote learning, without the presence of a teacher, does not replace daily instruction. We also knew that we could not expect parents to homeschool their children. Teachers provided students with engaging activities, assignments, and projects to maintain skills already taught.

Communication: Teachers communicated with families on a daily basis, providing weekly and/or daily assignments. Teachers were available for questions each day. Communication was via email, Google Classroom, phone, or videoconferencing (Google Hangout). Students heard from their special education teachers, related service providers, and tiered support teachers on an individual basis to help support their learning. Please note that our staff members were also managing through this health crisis with their own families and may have had young children at home.

For those families who struggled with Internet issues, hotspots were purchased and delivered to families to establish Wi-Fi connections in their neighborhood. Students were able to complete assignments and have Google Classroom meetings with their teachers.

A number of times the school resource officer went to the student's home to inform parents that although the buildings were closed, school was still open. Unfortunately, Child Protective Services had to be contacted for lack of student participation.

The governor decided to suspend all state testing. This created a new dilemma, especially for our graduating seniors who needed the Regents examination to graduate. After much confusion, the governor decided to waive all state examinations and students would be able to advance to the next grade without using New York State Assessment and Regents examinations. As a result, students were not penalized.

T. D.—Building Administrator, FL

Communication

Staff: From an administrator's view, the communication was inequitable. Teachers were in the dark about online learning mostly until the end of March. They were not brought in to discuss options, what would most benefit their students, and so on. They were given training the Friday before we were going live on Tuesday. Administration had some insight but not much more in advance of the teachers.

Parents/students: I personally sent out daily/weekly Remind messages to all the students/parents. I did send periodically emails through the system to the whole class but some students either chose to not check them or didn't remember or know they had email through myLearning. The district sent out monthly newsletters to parents, but there was no guarantee they were read. Some teachers communicated a lot with their students' others once a week, if at all.

Expectations

The expectations at first were just to get the students logged in and then to complete the work. It was so fast-paced and the district handled most of the decisions, so that administration, teachers, students, and parents were in the dark. The original thought was that this would only be for two weeks, but then it was extended for the rest of the school year and we had to make it work. Students didn't think fourth quarter counted because the governor said there would be no state assessments. Some students were familiar with the learning platform; others were not, which affected their success.

Assistance Given or Needed

There was little assistance given, but a lot was needed. Canvas, our virtual platform, could not give data by grade level, which affected how efficiently we could track students, especially those who struggled. Because it wasn't built this way, we couldn't adjust it to meet our new needs. Some of the reports that were supposed to be helpful to find which students were/weren't working, who was failing a course, and so on did not always pull the most accurate or updated data. The courses were uneven even in similar subject areas: one science class had fourteen assignments due the first fifteen days where others had one to three and some none at all.

Cooperation of Child/Teacher/Administration of School

Students cooperated as much as possible but there were some students who didn't do anything. As stated previously, some teachers communicated daily/

weekly with students via emails, announcements on the course homepage, and/or phone call/text messages home. Others did not communicate unless told to do so by administration.

Concerns on Reopening Options

We built the content and curriculum around the concept that whole classes and/or teachers will be out for weeks due to the virus, so authentic learning did not happen on campuses. Various virtual curriculums were available.

Socially distancing high schoolers in a classroom was not feasible because there were too many students in one room. New furniture was all tables to encourage collaboration. Therefore, students could not sit at a desk but had to sit in a chair with a book as their temporary desk.

Trying to keep students from congregating in the commons between classes, which is something all the upperclassmen have done for years, was difficult. Getting students to follow a walk pathway took time for training and directing.

TEACHERS

Nicole—Florida

Throughout the coronavirus pandemic, I had the unique opportunity to view the challenges from both the parental and educator perspectives. The anxiety that I had experienced in trying to make sense of something that we did not fully understand was stressful, as data surrounding the spread of the virus constantly changed.

As an educational leader, my mindset to facilitate learning for all students was precedent. The education of my three children was a paramount initiative for me during the last quarter of the 2019–2020 school year. The unprecedented events that led to the closing of schools concurrently turned me into a homeschooling parent a overnight. Trying to navigate online learning platforms for my children in three different elementary grade levels was a challenge that we met head on, as they accepted me as their teacher, while often resisting the changes in routine that were out of our control.

It was as if we were trying to create the vehicle of distance learning while we were driving it full steam ahead to conclude the school year. In addition to homeschooling through a virtual platform, my full-time job as a behavior specialist turned into a remote position that required attention and focus throughout the day. As I worked alongside administration and the rest of our student services team, we collaborated to ensure student support and problem-solving throughout the distance learning period. My heart was heavy upon hearing that many students were not participating in online learning, a result of the inequity in educational opportunities during this time.

For some students, lack of technology or access to information was a difficulty. For others, parental support was lacking and students struggled to complete learning assignments independently. I am grateful for the opportunity to educate my three children in a home that has Internet and access to digital devices to aid in their learning. I am thankful for the ability to feed and take care of my children during a time when many families are struggling to make ends meet.

Finally, I am thankful for my own education, which continues at this present time as I pursue my doctoral degree in educational leadership and my employment in one of the largest school districts in America. As educational leaders, we must continue to be vigilant in the application of policy to ensure the most equitable opportunities for all students. Reopening schools continues to be a topic of interest for Americans of all ages. My personal view is that since the infection rates are rising, we will most likely be educating students remotely in the fall, as I can't see how buses and school environments could be considered safe for students during a time when the virus is spreading rampantly. I was prepared to teach my children while supporting students and colleagues at my school site.

PARENTS

The reality for many was that they could not do their jobs from home while ensuring their children were consistently on target in their schooling, especially for young students in elementary school and students with disabilities. Parents reported various experiences from around the country. Below are some examples of parents and students from each level of public schools.

PRESCHOOL AND ELEMENTARY

Amanda—Parent of Two Young Children

We lived in Massachusetts and have a seven-year-old first-grader and a four-year-old who had been attending preschool two days per week. Both kids' schools shut down in mid-March. The preschooler's remote learning setup was pretty minimal and ended at the end of April. The preschool director shared a folder in Google Drive each week including a weekly theme, a few worksheets and ideas for activities, and a few short videos of some of the teachers reading stories.

We gave up pretty early on trying to stick with whatever weekly theme had been suggested as I figured out what kind of activities were likely to keep him engaged (we landed on working together on letter recognition/

writing practice and math practice during the times of day when his brother was working on the same subjects, plus a lots of reading and free play). I loved the idea of the teachers' read-aloud videos, but unfortunately they seemed to really confuse and upset him. The class tried a few Zoom "play-dates" early on, but those were a disaster.

I was happy with the level of communication from my first-grader's school. We received two Sunday night emails from his teacher each week: one with a personal video message from her to the students and one linking the week's remote learning spreadsheet. She also welcomed individual emails throughout the week and was quick to respond. We also got an email from the superintendent's office every Monday, Wednesday, and Friday with updates about bigger-picture district and state decisions.

It's worth noting that the school made Chromebooks and iPads available for sign out if families didn't have a device available for their student(s) to work on. We were incredibly lucky that I was available to work with the kids, so my husband and I haven't had to juggle two full-time jobs with suddenly having the kids home twenty-four hours a day. It was still pretty difficult to get a lot of academic work done on any given day. My first-grader is an intense guy under the best of circumstances, and my four-year-old is a four-year-old. We've gotten into a routine of some math, plenty of reading, some writing practice, and some online learning plus something extra (art, science, something the older guy has gotten interested in) every day, with lots of breaks for playing outside.

Kim—Parent of Three Young Children in Oregon

Communication

The school district that we lived in did a relatively good job of communicating from the beginning of the school closures. We were one of the first districts within our state to close, and shortly after the closure we started to receive email updates on next steps for virtual learning. It took the district a few weeks to determine what the distance learning model would like. Our week of spring break was factored into that time frame, and once the teachers came back from the break the first phase of our distance learning was put into place. Initially, we were instructed to use home laptops and electronic devices to connect, but within a week we were given the option to pick up the school-issued devices (iPads) due to all the applications, passwords, and so on already being uploaded and accessible.

We picked up our children's devices as soon as we were able to. The following week the school sent out a communication that they would like families to pick up their school-issued devices regardless of whether they had other device options at home to make the transition to distance learning as smooth as possible.

Once the decision was made on April 8, 2020, by the state of Oregon that school would be closed for the remainder of the year, they implemented a "soft start" similar to the first week of school and following that the distance learning instruction ramped up to focus on the essential learning they felt was necessary for the rest of the school year. We were provided communication on how to pick up our children's school supplies from the school. These supplies included supplemental workbooks, journals, STEAM supply kits, personal belongings, and art projects from the year. Our teachers were very supportive and personally dropped off devices and supplies to children's homes if their parents were unable to get to the school during the allotted pick-up times. These supplemental items were utilized for the assignments for the remainder of the school year.

Expectations

From the beginning of our distance learning journey, we felt that our district had reasonable expectations. This was a new model for both the teachers, students, and parents, and we never felt that there were unrealistic expectations for the children. There were recommended daily numbers of hours for each grade level. Our second grader and kindergartner were given assignments daily to fit within those recommendations. The teachers did their best to make the assignments and instruction as engaging as possible.

They were not held to a strict schedule and there weren't any repercussions if an assignment was not completed. Our second grader had a weekly virtual meeting with his teacher and classmates where she set the expectations for the week, had "facetime" with the kids, and gave them the opportunity to catch up with each other from the weekend. They celebrated birthdays and other occasions, and it gave them the opportunity to stay connected.

Assistance Given or Needed

The teachers and administration at our school did the best they could given the circumstances. Our children's teachers were both very much involved and reached out frequently to give us the opportunity to express any concerns and request feedback on what was and was not working. The district sent out a couple of surveys throughout the distance learning period to get a sense of accessibility to devices and Internet as well as parent input. We felt that given the circumstances our school did a fair job of communicating and providing support during an uncertain time.

Cooperation and Challenges

One of the biggest challenges of the distance learning model was the lack of preparation for both the school and the parents. The school closures as a result of COVID-19 happened so fast that the districts had no time to prepare and parents were suddenly thrown into unknown territory where they now had to juggle working from home, homeschooling, and being the caretaker for their school-aged and younger children—essentially three jobs compacted into one. When the school closures first started, there was a multitude of structured schedules to be found online, with each hour blocked off and confined to a certain activity—reading, math, craft time, free time, and so on.

We tried that, and it was fun and novel in our household for about three days, but the novelty wore off quickly. Once you factor in work obligations and juggling the demands of an active toddler, any sort of schedule was quickly thrown out the window. In the end we were simply trying to carve out a few hours each day to complete assignments and make sure the kids got their reading time in.

Personally, I had little insight into their day-to-day traditional learning prior to the stay at home orders, aside from the small glimpse we receive during parent–teacher conferences and what little information I could glean out of them when their school day was done. We found ourselves trying to pick up where the teachers had left off, and that was uncharted territory that we didn't feel equipped to deal with. We were constantly torn between wanting to provide our children the freedom to learn other life skills and making sure that this time was not a stressful one for their emotional well-being and the feeling of guilt that we weren't doing enough and that they would fall behind.

Brett—Parent of Young Child from North Carolina

Communication

This was a bit of a challenge at first. Everything happened really quickly and it was tough to manage the massive amounts of email from my work (Duke Health and Duke University) and the Montessori program. It would have been more easily absorbed if the emails stated clearly when they decided to shut down and then that they would come up with a plan by "x" date. Instead, both systems sent out numerous emails with little pieces of information and tasks to complete. Given the situation, I think they did well, but I thought this was one big area that could have improved. As time went on and we got further into the pandemic, the school did well with communication about how and when we could come and pick up various supplies they were providing for different lessons we could complete with our kids.

Expectations

From the Montessori school, there were none. Being that his class was a modified preschool/daycare, they told us we could choose to participate in any parts that we wanted to as we were able. They were very understanding that everyone's home life would have unique characteristics and they did not want the preschool to be a stressor for parents or children.

The school provided multiple avenues for us to continue learning through various websites that I assume they paid for a subscription to. The websites had books that could be read online or could be read to the child online from a prerecording. The school also supplied us with various cutout learning activities similar to the 3D learning activities they have in the classroom.

School and administration were very cooperative. Bryce did fairly well with class, but we only had thirty minutes of class each day (it was a very valuable thirty minutes, as I was able to get some things done around the house during this time). At first, he needed reminders to sit and stay involved with his class; however, after a week or two he was engaged most of each class with very little direction from me. When he did get distracted, it was normally toward the end of class, so I am not sure if they could have held his attention much longer if they tried. It would have been nice to have an additional learning opportunity a couple of times throughout the day, but it is understandable since no one was really prepared for this whole mess.

Overall, I was pretty happy with the experience and the school moved quickly to make the best out of a difficult situation. However, in my opinion this does not seem to be a good long-term model for children this young.

MIDDLE AND HIGH SCHOOL

Rita—Parent from California

As a parent of a senior—a senior with an IEP since the age of three—the final year of school was looked forward to with both excitement and relief. School has been a struggle through the years and adding the changes due to COVID made this final year of high school sad. We are nothing, however, if not resilient and we got on board with the plans the school arranged for the end of the school year. We ensured our senior was set up for online classes. We tried to keep him engaged during the "extra credit" period (post spring break—class resumption at the end of April), but most importantly we ensured we were ready for school to start at the end of April, as the school stated would occur.

I understand this was a big change for the school and for their teachers, and we worked with a schedule of having one one-hour class per week per class; however, the teachers were not conducting classes, even though these teachers already had online systems to provide classwork and interact with students. It was apparent that some teachers were not providing any assignments outside of the "busy work" provided by the school district to keep students engaged during the month of April. Obviously, these teachers would have had a learning plan for their classes for the end of the year—and those learning plans seem to have disappeared completely. When I questioned one teacher on whether he was planning on conducting ANY classes, he stated that he didn't expect his seniors to show up because their grades couldn't go down and there was a "no fault" clause for teachers, even if they didn't conduct a class.

While as a senior he would have been happy to end his school year as of spring break, as his parent, I wanted to ensure he completed his education. The actions of the different teachers was very inconsistent in their approach and left both my child and I confused on what should or shouldn't be done. Thankfully, we were fortunate in having resource teachers who went over and above keeping my son engaged, keeping up with the class work and ensuring he continued to get an education during the last 2.5 months of the school year!

In speaking with other people within the school district, they experienced similar issues. I am aware of one child whose grades went down at the end of the school year. Different teachers would count attendance differently. Some teachers stated that grades were dependent on attendance. The inconsistencies and the attitudes of some teachers were a FAR CRY from what the school district was advertising about conducting online classes, and this was an extremely disappointing end to my child's education.

Sarah—Parent from Florida

To be fair to the administrators and educators, what we experienced during the fourth quarter of the 2019–2020 school year was not distance learning but crisis learning. The district quickly implemented mandatory online distance learning. It was very cookie cutter, but it kept the kids' minds working in some capacity. For that I am grateful.

I am the mother of a middle school and high school boy. They had very differing opinions on distant learning. My MSB (middle school boy) loved it. He missed the social side of school but loved the freedom to log on and check the boxes each day. He had to utilize the three chances rule since no one was teaching him the material. We had a requirement in our house that you could do a "lesson" twice by yourself, and if you did not receive an "A," then headmaster mom would sit down and teach you the lesson before taking the assessment for the third and final time. My MSB has seven different teachers. Math, dance, and Spanish were the only ones offering weekly Zooms, and he attended each of them.

Our thought was even if you don't have a question about the material, it is a good temperature check. He ended the fourth quarter with straight As for the first time. He checked boxes and completed assignments, although I am not sure how much he truly learned. My MSB's teachers were very responsive when he reached out for help. He was able to communicate with them privately via Google Voice and email.

My HSB (high school boy) is a whole other story. He was a straight A student taking mostly honors and AP classes. He is also a three-sport athlete. He absorbed information from verbal learning. He loved discussion and debate. He did not enjoy distant learning. My HSB learned quickly that even with a rubric, teachers grade differently. He had six different teachers and during the fourth quarter any teacher in a specific subject area (minus AP classes) grades assignments. He was self-motivated and ended the semester with straight As but did have two Bs for the fourth quarter.

He truly missed the in-class instruction and discussion. I believed that any relationships he built with his teachers was lost over distance learning. When Zooms were offered, he attended them, but other than his AP class that was very rare.

Administration for both my MSB and HSB was very good about communication. As a parent I was given many outlets to gain information. It was my responsibility to utilize those platforms: social media, remind texts, automated calls.

SUMMARY

As you can see from the experiences shared by administrators, teachers, and parents, there were many challenges contributing to educational leader's responsibilities during the pandemic crisis. The issues of leadership needed and learned through the experience of a global pandemic were the epitome of leading during crises.

Throughout the chapters of the book, additional experiences will be shared by practitioners and other stakeholders, as they contribute greatly to the conversation of what leaders need to facilitate and manage during any and all crises.

Leadership requires knowledge, skill, communication, transparency, and relationships with stakeholders. Integrity, resiliency, and compassion are all components of ethical and practical leaders (Hegarty & Moccia, 2018). Organizational leaders make difficult choices and decisions on behalf of their clients, the people they serve. The components of ethical leadership assist leaders in creating a systemic framework that supports the organization during crisis management.

Educational leaders engage others in the work of the schools, districts, and organizations that they lead. Stakeholders who trust the leaders, based on ethical engagement of practice, are best able to serve their organizations during typical events and crises events (Engelbrecht et al., 2014). Modeling attributes of ethical leadership impacts employees who follow the behaviors exhibited by organizational leaders. This systemic approach allows the development of consistent practice that contributes to the culture of the organization (Al Halbusi et al., 2019).

If a strong, collaborative culture of an organization exists, stakeholders will collectively deal with success and challenges. Value-based leadership, as defined by Cohen (2005), identified a three-step process in creating a positive climate for change, engaging the whole organization, and implementing sustainable change protocols. This practice enables a positive culture to support leadership applicable to leading during crises.

Issues of school safety and school shootings were priorities after multiple school shootings between 1999 (Columbine) and the school shootings in Sandy Hook, Connecticut (2012) and Parkland, Florida (2018). Educational and community leaders developed multiple plans of action as a result. Now the priority has shifted to health concerns. However, as a result of the changes due to the COVID-19 pandemic, important issues of financial security, resource allocation, mental health concerns, isolation, and fear impacting communities and community stakeholders emerged, similar to the issues surrounding school shootings and school safety.

The key difference during this crisis is that all schools and school districts in every state were impacted. Thankfully, if a school shooting occurs, it has been a tragic event in one school at a time.

During the pandemic, police brutality, social injustice, and racial inequity issues became focused upon after the murders of George Floyd and others at the hands of police authorities. The resulting movement of Black Lives Matter, civil rights protests, and racial challenges impacted school leaders and challenged their considerations for incorporating the meaning of these social movements into the classroom. Some educators expressed concerns that after months of being isolated from others in schools, some children, when school resumed, would bring misunderstandings and obtuse messages to their classrooms. How educators facilitated conversations around acceptance of others and negated some of those negative experiences were shared concerns of teachers and school administrators.

In subsequent chapters of this book, additional voices from the field will be shared, with the intent of providing a basis for moving forward. Strategies and opportunities for supporting change in a unique national situation, how attributes impact schools at a local level, and what considerations of crisis management and leadership are discussed and shared.

REFERENCES

Aefsky, F., ed. (2019). *Can we ensure safe schools? A collaborative guide on focused strategies for school safety.* Rowman & Littlefield.

Al Halbusi, H., Ismail, M., & Omar, S. (May 2019). Examining the impact of ethical leadership on employees ethical behavior. *Journal of Technology Management and Business, 6*(2), 389–98.

Bender, L. (March 2020). Key messages and actions for COVID-19 prevention and control in schools. UNICEF New York.

Engelbrecht, A., Heine, G., & Mahembe, B. (2014). The influence of ethical leadership on trust and work engagement. *SA Journal of Industrial Psychology, 40*(1), 1–9.

Hegarty, N., & Moccia, S. (2018). Components of ethical leadership and their importance in sustaining organizations over the long term. *Journal of Values-Based Leadership, 11*(1), 1–10.

Chapter 2

Crisis Management in a Pandemic: Voices from the Field

Renee Sedlack

As instructional leaders, principals are prepared to implement, monitor, and evaluate academic programs, innovative initiatives, and tiered systems approaches to address various needs of students and the development of professional learning communities to enhance the skills and abilities of teachers. Along with this major responsibility, principals are also asked to maintain the health and safety of hundreds, perhaps thousands, of students and staff. Most importantly, they are expected to develop, practice, and implement well-practiced plans when crises occur on their campuses. This nation has seen numerous school shootings and weather-related disasters; each of these instances required crisis management to unexpected levels.

The principal's role in helping staff, students, and families during natural disasters is incredibly important (Harris, 2006). Understanding the impact that events have on others is essential for enabling the work to continue in new ways and in uncertain conditions. Recognizing individual needs, prioritizing work for successful implementation, communicating in ways that are familiar to stakeholders, and asking for help when needed are key ingredients for success.

At the same time, principals need to be anticipating and planning for what may come next (Reich, 2020). It is important to take time to step away from the current crisis and plan for a variety of potential outcomes in the future.

Recently, principals across the nation faced a crisis for which there was no written plan, no practiced drills, and no widely developed and tested emergency management procedures.

During the spring of 2020, nearly 40 million K-12 public school students across the country were out of school due to COVID-19. As a result, school principals were playing a pivotal role in ensuring that student learning would continue. In many areas of the United States, schools provide necessary mental health and emotional supports students have come to rely on in the traditional school structure (Superville, 2020). For a significant portion of the population, food insecurity is a concern. Children who are not in school miss the two meals they can count on each day. The loss of the traditional school setting impacted students beyond academics.

The role of the school principal changed as a result of this worldwide pandemic and facilitating change in the light of a multitude of unknown factors was a challenge many have never faced. Experts in the field suggest that principals, especially in times of crisis, depend on what leaders know is best practice along with the commitment to self-care (Center for Creative Leadership, 2020).

Leading others to work in new ways when they themselves are experiencing personal trauma presented a unique challenge. Leaders need to remember that everyone who is observing or living through a crisis views it through a unique lens and that reactions to change and ability to implement new ways to work may be a struggle (Center for Creative Leadership, 2020).

Recognizing and managing the emotions of all stakeholders in the situation can help develop the resiliency and power of the group. Treating people with consideration and genuine concern, paying attention, listening, and responding to what people are telling you are key behaviors. It is essential to consider what is not being said as well (Center for Creative Leadership, 2020).

Leaders with a positive outlook and who have a foundation of relational trust with a variety of stakeholders will often be able to facilitate movement through a crisis by building in the talents, leadership, and expertise of those within the school.

While principals need to be accessible, clear communicators, problem solvers, and caregivers for their school family and their own, it is essential that principals care for themselves as well.

> By paying attention to your own emotions, needs, and behaviors, you will be better prepared to handle the human dimensions of the crisis. As a result, you will be more capable of containing the crisis, regaining control, minimizing damage, and effectively preventing, defusing, and reducing the duration of an extremely difficult leadership situation. (Center for Creative Leadership, 2020)

So how did principals lead their communities through a challenge unlike any other? Let's hear from voices in the field as principals tell their personal stories.

PRIORITIES DURING THE PANDEMIC: FOR THIS PRINCIPAL IT'S PERSONAL—LATOYA JORDAN, ELEMENTARY

Prior to COVID-19, increasing student achievement in reading and maintaining student enrollment were two of the major challenges at Lacoochee Elementary. Lacoochee Elementary serves approximately 320 students in grades pre-K-5. Lacoochee is a Title I school in which 95 percent of the students receive free and reduced-price lunch. The school has historically struggled with maintaining academic excellence; the current high school graduation rate for students who attended Lacoochee Elementary is approximately 25 percent. Transitioning to a virtual learning environment due to COVID-19 presented unique challenges due to the nature of our community and student population.

After we began distance learning and started to talk about student engagement, we noticed there were students who reported having Internet (based on the survey) who had not engaged in distance learning. Upon learning that nearly 30 percent of the families had no Internet or were using something that was either inconsistent or potentially costly, we made exceptions for those families.

Even though distance learning is not a new concept, in the case of this pandemic, families did not have the option to choose if this would be the best learning environment for their child. The current national crisis dictated where we are in education. Although district and school personnel had very little time to plan, both groups worked tirelessly to provide students with quality education.

It is critical that school leaders know their school community. Knowing and understanding my families allowed me to be proactive when planning to address their needs. Although the challenges were magnified with the loss of instruction, this experience showed me that during stressful times it is extremely important that educators understand that our priorities are not the same as what families prioritize.

IMPACT OF COVID-19: LOSING THE CHANCE TO SAY GOODBYE—CARIN HETZLER-NETTLES, MIDDLE/HIGH SCHOOL

Major challenges prior to COVID-19 were managing grades 6–12, and all of the activities that come with both the middle and high school levels. I was one principal, responsible for all seven grade levels, overseeing a staff of over 200 and an administrative team of six assistant principals.

The challenges transitioning to virtual learning as a result of the pandemic were that we did not have physical access to our staff, communication in the midst of uncertainty, maintaining a sense of humor, hope, grit, and perseverance, and getting devices into the hands of our students and families. Our staff left for spring break, and we've never all been physically on campus since. That was a big thing to immediately have to adjust to—the virtual way of work and wrapping your brain around not seeing everyone for an unspecified amount of time.

Communication is key in a crisis. We had some exceptional processes in place at CCMHS already, so we really didn't have to change the way we communicated. Our way of work is our Howler Hub, which is a weekly digital staff newsletter that I publish each Friday. Our staff is used to receiving this Hub, and they know that any and all information is put into it weekly.

We immediately began pushing all of the important information we gathered from the district and putting it in that one place for our staff. We had to send a few additional Howler Hubs at the beginning of the COVID-19 crisis, but our staff always have appreciated the "one-stop shopping" of having the Hub. We were able to channel any and all communications coming from our district, could highlight great ideas from our staff, and could keep our entire school team abreast of everything they needed to know regarding the COVID-19 crisis and distance learning. I have always felt that our weekly hub was valuable, but in this crisis it was an exceptional way to communicate without overwhelming everyone with emails.

As a leader, my job was to constantly think about other people. How will my decisions or the decisions of others affect those who work with me and how will those decisions affect my students? As a leader, oftentimes those thoughts overwhelm your mind, and you stop thinking of yourself. Selflessness is good in leadership, but during a pandemic, or crisis of any kind, it is important to carve time out for yourself to digest what is occurring in the world and the affects it has on you personally.

I have found it very difficult to "read a room" via Zoom. This came into play on a few occasions during distance learning, and mostly with my assistant principals. I learned quickly to do a little pulse check at the beginning of the meeting. We used this when we were physically on our campus prior to any meeting; as we are a Trauma Informed Care School, it is called a "Community Meeting."

Device deployment was another large challenge. Our community fluctuated between 42 percent and 47 percent of students who are eligible for free or reduced-price meals. It was difficult for us to wrap our brains around giving away electronic devices, but we made a plan and got it accomplished. We were concerned that we wouldn't have enough devices, but we actually had plenty for our community. My team came together and overcame many obstacles and worked very well with our staff to finish the school year strong.

Our school district's response to the pandemic was outstanding. We have an exceptional online school called Pasco eSchool, and the principal who runs that school is an amazing leader. She basically took her template and taught all of us (elementary, middle, and high administrators and teachers) how to be "virtual" administrators and teachers. She and our district leaders charted a course for distance learning that gave us all focus and immediate information.

This leadership was essential in getting our students and families everything they needed in an incredibly quick fashion. As principals we weren't each doing our own thing at our individual sites; we truly worked as a cohesive unit and as a district to do what was best for our students and families. The response of the district allowed me to clearly and transparently communicate with my staff via our Howler Hub. A "direction" is essential in this type of emergency. There are so many unanswered questions in the world, so any type of direction and normalcy is needed and appreciated by employees and families.

We assigned all students who struggle academically, behaviorally, or whose families are in economic crisis to case managers and secretarial staff to check in via the phone every week during distance learning. By reaching out to so many families, we continued to build relationships with families through distance learning. We showed our families and our students that relationships are key and most important to us as a school family.

I learned much about myself and what advice I would share with those who are aspiring leaders. Each incident that you experience makes you stronger and a better leader. Each incident teaches you new things about yourself and those who surround you. This brought to light, once again, the importance of a school in its community.

BUILDING COMPASSIONATE CONNECTIONS: UNEXPECTED OPPORTUNITIES IN A PANDEMIC—ED LAROSE, MIDDLE SCHOOL

When we were faced with the onset of COVID-19, our focus changed. Our major challenge with transitioning to the virtual environment was staying in communication with our families. Throughout the virtual platform, being able to reach families for reasons such as picking up devices to working from home, signing up with their classes, staying active within classes, and picking up/dropping off packets for those who did not have Internet were all reasons to reach out to families.

Our school staff ran into a few roadblocks when attempting to communicate with families—incorrect phone numbers, full voice mailboxes, and parents upset about receiving calls and refusing to talk with us. As the principal, I attempted to visit as many homes as I could. I brought families the devices and packets they needed and attempted to visit families we were not successfully reaching through email or phone. The visits were successful in small doses, but overall the list grew too large for families that required a visit.

Throughout the final quarter of the school year, I was able to meet with the entire staff all at once and then meet with each department as well through the use of Microsoft Teams. We spoke about compassion from the very beginning of the pandemic when working with students and thinking about our families. The staff made the decision as a whole to not let any student fail the last quarter due to the virtual platform. I think as a staff we arrived at that decision due to the continuous communication and meetings we had throughout the quarter and sharing what others within our school, school district, and state were advocating in regards to instructional practices.

When I reflect about what I could have done differently, several thoughts come to mind. I think building a tiered support system for multiple areas of concern and having the correct number of people within each tiered support could have been organized more effectively. I am always looking for ways to protect my staff from extra tasks, and I believe doing so in this situation backfired a bit due to the number of concerns that quickly arose. A tiered support with multiple people involved would have allowed me to work more efficiently and effectively.

I learned much about myself and my role as a leader during this challenging time. As leaders, we must continue to communicate as often and as timely as possible, especially as we continue to walk through uncharted times. Staff, students, and families need to be updated and communicated to in a proactive manner whenever possible. In retrospect, it would have been beneficial once the pandemic occurred to have scheduled updates, so stakeholders would know when information would be disseminated. When I managed hurricane shelters in the past (this is part of a principal's job description in Hernando County), there is always a set time and location where updates are posted. I believe all stakeholders involved would have benefited from this approach.

In the beginning of this reflection I talked about the challenges my school faced before the onset of the pandemic. I spoke about parent involvement as being a challenge prior to COVID. I do believe many of our families became closer and more supportive of the school, the teachers, and their individual students' academic process. I am hopeful that the setting that was forced upon our schools and families will lead into more family support when the students are at school but more importantly at home when the student is continuing his/her academic studies.

MEETING THE PANDEMIC CHALLENGE: MORE THAN TEACHING AND LEARNING—JULIE MARKS, ELEMENTARY

Chester W. Taylor Elementary School (CWTES) is a Title I school. We serve roughly 650 students in pre-K through fifth grade with approximately 83 percent of students eligible for free and reduced-price meals. CWTES serves mostly a rural population with generational poverty.

Prior to the pandemic, attendance at CWTES was a concern along with meeting the social and emotional needs of all students; we have many students moving in who speak little or no English. Attendance has always been a concern at CWTES. We strive to develop attractive attendance initiatives and work with our families to understand the importance of not just coming to school but attending from start to finish. We experience a lot of tardiness and early checkouts as well. We have an attendance plan in place and we use our social worker to assist with families who struggle to send their children to school.

This year was also a year that we had an influx of students coming to our school speaking another language. In some instances, we registered four students in one day who only spoke Spanish. With only one English language learners (ELL) instructional assistant, she was stretched thin. We began using additional support staff to teach our students English beginning with the basic alphabet, power words, and beginning phonics and phonemic awareness strategies.

And then came the pandemic.

If someone told me that I would be opening a virtual school in three days, I would have laughed. Thank goodness our district did the legwork on the curriculum for our teachers, so we could focus on the student and staff needs at the school level. One of the first challenges of transitioning into the virtual learning world was making sure all students had devices and Internet access. Due to the rural location in which some of our students live, an Internet connection was not an option for them.

Our teachers did a fantastic job gathering information from our families to see what their needs were as far as devices and Internet. They were able to connect with over 90 percent of our families in less than two days while the office staff followed up with the other 10 percent. We knew who needed devices within a three-day period. Once we knew what we needed, we began collecting, cleaning, and organizing devices to go out. We issued well over 250 devices in two days. Throughout the pandemic, we continued to give out devices and assist with Internet issues on a weekly basis. The first two weeks of distance learning, especially in the early grades, were spent on assisting with technology issues and not as much on learning.

The learning curve for all staff, students, and families was intense and exhausting. Teachers in the early grades were overwhelmed with compassion fatigue at first. They were working more with the parents than with the students in the beginning. Parents had lost jobs, were overwhelmed with the system, had more than one child, and did not have the knowledge to help and many expressed their own stress with our staff. Being compassionate educators, they empathized and listened, and it put stress on them as teachers. Many of the teachers were not comfortable with virtual learning yet either, and they too had their own children at home. Administration did our best to reach out and support, but when you don't see or talk to them every day, you truly don't know how they are doing.

Teachers in the upper grades worked hard to get students to turn in work and get on Zoom meetings. We wanted to be sure to be compassionate while also having expectations that school was still in session. The hardest part was the grading. In a time like this, you have to put your own personal philosophies aside and think about what families are going through to just download, complete, and upload an assignment.

Watching my own middle and high school children do this the first time was difficult, so asking elementary families to do it and then give them a poor grade could be discouraging. For the first several weeks, we graded for completion only. We started by giving them full credit with feedback. As the weeks went on, we began to focus more on the content. This seemed to work best for our school given the circumstances.

Another challenge that we faced was with our families that spoke another language. With only one English language learners instructional assistant, she was spending hours on the phone helping parents, students, and teachers. We had to think outside the box and recruit another instructional assistant who spoke Spanish and assign her families as well. They both became liaisons between the school and families throughout the entire process. They helped parents get on Zoom, download apps, navigate the system, translate with the teachers, and be an overall support for both families and teachers.

As with any school that has a high population of students in poverty, we worried about them all the time. Our district began a feeding site on our campus, but families that I knew needed support were not coming to pick up food. Our social worker and I would pack our cars up and make deliveries as well, just to be sure students were eating. Families welcomed us to their homes, were appreciative of us, and in some cases cried, as they did not have transportation to the school for the food.

In the beginning, we were highly focused on making sure students had devices and access to Internet. One thing that I wish we had done differently from the beginning was set up a better way to communicate across the school. Many people were making phone calls, sending texts, emails, and so on, including our learning design coach, administration, office staff, instructional assistants, and teachers. Everyone was keeping track of the way they were communicating, but it wasn't being housed all in one spot.

Chester W. Taylor has a very strong, dedicated group of teachers. The leadership team is dynamite and had truly led the school and their teams through this transition. We were able to continue to have strong weekly PLCs as well as school-based leadership meetings and school intervention team (SIT) meetings.

Through this process, I have had some personal ups and downs. The first week was truly a challenge that I accepted. It gave me energy to think that we had to convert our brick-and-mortar school into a virtual school in less than a week. I was energized and was the cheerleader for the team. I am a strategic thinker, so I started thinking about roles of teachers, team facilitators, instructional assistants, administration, office staff, and so on.

I pulled my leadership team together and told them to look out for one another; I told them of my sadness and the emptiness I felt in week three and to be ready for it as well. I asked them to let their teams know to walk away, stick to their "office hours," don't work on the weekends, and figure out how to get up and move, as we are not used to sitting in front of a computer like many industries do. Working from home can take a toll on you. You can get up and start working at 8:00 and not stop until midnight if you aren't careful.

I tried to connect with my leadership team and assistant principal as much as possible, but at this time of the year there is also a lot of decision making for the next year. We were in the midst of making Title I decisions, allocations were getting released, an extended school year was being discussed, teacher appreciation week was upon us, and we were trying to still have end-of-year activities to keep going all while the unknown was there for all of us.

WHITEWATER RAFTING IN THE AGE OF CORONAVIRUS—RIC MELLIN, HIGH SCHOOL PRINCIPAL

Land O' Lakes High School is located in central Florida. We serve students from grade 9 through 12. Once a rural community, Land O' Lakes has transformed into a popular bedroom community for Tampa.

One-quarter of our population are considered economically disadvantaged. Just over 1 percent are English language learners, 10 percent are students with disabilities, and within that percentage are students that are in a self-contained program for emotional behavior disorders. We have an international baccalaureate (IB) program and Advanced Placement (AP) courses, and each year we graduate between 400 and 500 students. Our graduation rate was 94.4 percent for the class of 2019.

Many of the major challenges that we face are similar to our colleagues in other high schools. We need to prepare and support them for the different end-of-course assessments and graduation-requirement tests that occur.

Although we provide support for testing through our delivery of instruction, many teachers do begin to focus more on testing during the second semester. The month of May is booked solid with student testing.

We administer well over 10,000 tests in that month, including IB exams, AP exams, in-school SAT test, state end-of-course exams, English assessments, CTE certification exams, and district finals. As you can imagine, each test has its own set of criteria that creates tremendous burdens on the school.

Prior to the onset of the pandemic crisis, the test coordinators were creating schedules for each of the exams that needed to be administered. It is a multifaceted assignment that takes a very long time to develop. This means that we spend an intense amount of time dealing with different types of offenses. We were also conducting final preparations for end-of-year celebrations, field trips, and events. Club sponsors, activity directors, coaches, and parents all coordinated with our bookkeeper to make sure that paperwork and funds were all in place.

When we heard that schools would not reopen, it created a tremendous burden on the bookkeeper. All of the contracts had to be renegotiated or canceled. In many cases, this required having to address no refund policies. Luckily, because this was a worldwide event, most businesses provided full reimbursements that have resulted in well over 1,000 refund checks back to our students.

The transition to a virtual learning environment happened very quickly. We went on spring break hoping that we would return to our building in one week. The governor made an announcement that all schools will be closed for two weeks. Then it was extended, and finally the decision that we would remain away through the remainder of the school year.

Because many of our course offerings are AP and IB, we had to contract with our own staff to prepare course work. Through Zoom meetings we were able to conference with all of the advanced course teachers. We discussed the type of content that they should be covering during the fourth quarter. AP teachers usually spend the fourth quarter in test-preparation mode.

We discovered that the College Board was going to be moving their tests online. New test specifications were communicated to schools, and we began to rethink how to prepare students for this new challenge. Students frequently met with teachers through Zoom, telephone conversations, or other communication techniques within the Canvas platform. Preparations changed a bit since the College Board would be allowing students to use notes and other learning aids.

Tests were all moved online, so we had to make sure that all students had access to a device. In addition, the time on task was shortened. Constant messages were sent to students and families through Canvas, email, social media, our telephone messaging system, and posts on our website. Ensuring that every student still had an opportunity to test at home and provide an environment where they could succeed was paramount.

IB changed their requirements during the pandemic. Seniors who would have been required to pass exams to earn an IB diploma now would be required to just submit an acceptable extended essay. Teachers quickly adapted to these new expectations and spent most of the fourth quarter ensuring that the seniors submitted a quality assignment.

Because three-quarters of our student population are from middle- or upper-class homes, we did not have a problem with students having a device to start distance learning. Communications were distributed to ensure that those who needed any device had one to start their coursework immediately. We scheduled a day when students could visit the school to receive a laptop computer.

Over 200 devices were handed out while observing current CDC guidelines to protect those who were involved. We also have given out mobile hotspots to families that do not have good connectivity. Throughout the time that we have been using the virtual platform, administrators and teachers have been monitoring student completion of work. A system was utilized that identified those who were falling behind.

I was fortunate to have some excellent professors and role models who have molded me into the school leader that I have become. Having spent the last twenty-five years in schools as both a teacher and an administrator provided me with experiences that are invaluable. It has served me well to adopt many of the strategies that bode well in any educational environment or during a crisis.

At the start of every school year, I tell the story to our faculty and staff that a school year in a high school is similar to a whitewater rafting trip. If you've ever taken one of these excursions, you know that everything is carefully mapped out ahead of time by the guide to ensure that safety measures are followed. It's important to know what you are going to come up against and to have goals and objectives that have been thought about prior to reaching each set of rapids. Once the boat is put in the water and everybody sits in his or her place, it is very difficult to stop.

As the boat makes its way down the river, everyone has a job to do; yet there is usually very little time to prepare for what is in store. The pace and action are very quick, and those in the boat are rowing at the commands given by the guide. By the time you get an opportunity to stop and reflect on what happened, it's usually at the end of the trip.

A school year is very similar. Once the students enter the building on the first day, we have very little opportunity to stop and reflect on the goals that we set forth prior to their return. We usually don't get a chance for reflective time until our school year ends. The summer is our chance to summarize what just happened and prepare for the next school year.

The pandemic crisis gave us an opportunity to pull the boat over with some time to spare. We met to discuss what our students need in order to be successful. We talked about compassion and grace.

During distance learning, our staff tempered their expectations and were addressing things with an open mind. Many times a principal is stuck being the manager and disciplinarian. We don't get a chance to truly enjoy the school environment and the people who make up the organization. I've tried to spend time getting to know our seniors by connecting through meetings, messaging, and social media posts.

Connecting to families seemed to be the hardest thing that we dealt with during this crisis. It's difficult to know whether there truly is a disconnect or if they had a laissez-faire attitude about their child's education. Knowing that we would be away for so long, I would have pushed to have better means of communicating with families.

We certainly could have given our teachers more training regarding an online platform if we knew that it would play out so prominently in the work that we needed to do. In addition, the current scenario had some of our staff with job responsibilities that they could not do from home.

Early on in my studies to become an administrator, one of the best bits of advice that I received from someone was the phrase "let me get back to you." In schools things happen very rapidly, and many people want answers quickly. As a school leader, it can be very difficult to maneuver through all of the requests that you receive in a given day. And many of those questions warrant an immediate response, but you can risk making a poor decision by communicating an answer without thoroughly vetting all of the possibilities.

It's okay to let somebody know that you need to do more investigation before answering. Some might think that it's a sign of weakness to not offer an immediate response, but in the long run you can save yourself a lot of issues by spending time up front to ensure that you make the right decision.

Working remotely affords you the opportunity to really work through situations that are brought to your attention. It may be difficult to deal with some of the new circumstances that we faced, but it's better to slow down and look at all of the possibilities prior to committing an answer.

Prior to the pandemic I knew that I was a traditional, dependable, organized, procedural, and conventional administrator. However, during this crisis, the school needed a leader who was more compassionate, empathetic, devoted, inspirational, and sympathetic toward what families are facing. When things return back to normal, it's going to be important for me to remember that a true school leader leaves themselves open and vulnerable for people to see many different and important personality traits.

Being a building administrator for over twenty years builds a sense of confidence and knowledge toward how to deal with any situation that you come across. However, the COVID-19 pandemic brought on one of the most complex sets of circumstances that any of us has ever come across. In perspective, I believe that we're going to be coming out of this much more skilled, organized, and determined than ever to educate our children in a world that requires frequent adaptations. And that is OK.

So what lies ahead for our school principals? This excerpt from a recent publication of the New York City Leadership Academy offers an accurate perspective:

> We may not know exactly when school will return to school buildings, but we do know that when it does, disparities will be greater. Some of our students will have experienced hunger, trauma, discrimination, and loss of learning, while others will have had an enriching homeschooling experience. Create active plans to ensure that every student returns academically and emotionally whole.
> Partner with parents and consider how you can shift your practice in ways that will extend well beyond this crisis. (Grossman, 2020)

As school leaders across the country plan for the future, there is much uncertainty as to how the school years ahead will look for our nation's children, teachers, parents, and principals. As options are considered, school leaders must think creatively about instructional routines, health and safety of both staff and students, community building, food service, and mental health counseling (Reich, 2020). Managing this crisis may continue for years to come.

Most school leaders emerge at the end of their careers having had to navigate their schools through times of profound trauma that affect the entire community (Lehmann, 2020). These voices from the field attest to the strength, wisdom, and courage that school leaders demonstrated during one of most challenging crises in our nation's history.

REFERENCES

Center for Creative Leadership. (2020). How to lead through a crisis. https://blog.nassp.org/2020/01/22/leading-through-crisis/.

Grossman, J. (2020). We will support your leadership though COVID 19. *New York City Leadership Academy.* https://www.nycleadershipacademy.org/blog/we-will-support-your-leadership-through-the-covid-19-crisis.

Harris, Sandra. (2006). BRAVO principals: Help staff and students cope with stress. *Education World*. https://www.educationworld.com/a_admin/columnists/BRAVO/BRAVO007.shtml.

Lehmann, C. (January 2020). Leading through crisis. *National Association of School Principals*. https://blog.nassp.org/2020/01/22/leading-through-crisis/.

Reich, Justin. (2020). A crisis management system for educational leaders. *Education Week*. https://www.edweek.org/ew/articles/2020/04/24/a-crisis-management-system-for-education-leaders.html.

Superville, D. (2020). There is no guidebook: Being the principal in the age of coronavirus. *Education Week* (vol. 39, no. 32). https://blogs.edweek.org/edweek/District_Dossier/2020/03/principals_coronavirus_sel_teaching.html.

Chapter 3

Leadership Supporting Teachers, Students, and Families during Crises

Melinda Carver

LEADERSHIP CONSIDERATIONS

Temporary localized school closures as a result of health or natural emergencies occurred frequently for short periods of time; however, "the global scale and speed of the current educational disruption is unparalleled and, if prolonged, could threaten the right to education" (McCarthy, 2020, para. 3). The COVID-19 crisis of 2020 had a significant impact on educational systems and leaders.

ABC News reported on March 6 that 290 million students' educations had been disrupted worldwide by the COVID-19 virus (McCarthy, 2020). About a week later, on March 13, the World Economic Forum reported that over 421 million children had been affected by school closures in thirty-nine countries. They commented that the number did not include those students who are impacted by more localized school closures happening in another twenty-two countries (Tam & El-Azar, 2020).

In an attempt to support children, school leaders had to provide instruction through multiple mediums. Educators did what good teachers have always done, going above and beyond to meet the needs of their students. Instruction was provided online, through paper packets, at safe social distances, and in whatever way available. A picture of a teacher with his whiteboard demonstrating to a student through her closed glass storm door how to do her math work is just one example. Another teacher expressed her ideas this way: "Every child in every school deserves an equal education. A zip code and a neighborhood shouldn't dictate the quality of life a kid has. I need to know my kids are in a safe place, a place where they're being cared for, growing, and developing every day. Every child I teach deserves honor and respect." Educators everywhere are attempting to do what is right for children.

The experience in Duval County, Florida, helps illustrate the magnitude of the problem faced by each school district throughout the United States. In just three days, the county made the decision to close schools. In less than seventy-two hours, the transition team moved the entire district to an at-home, virtual instruction model while planning the mobilization of meal programs, distribution of technology equipment, provision of online teacher training, and a myriad of issues that come with the monumental change. During those three days, they created, printed, and distributed about 5 million pages of instructional content, loaded classes and content onto an online platform, gathered online resources, and trained about 8,000 teachers to teach virtually. Then they conducted a survey of technology needs for their 130,000 students and readied thousands of computers for student use. Then they prepped for neighborhood delivery of school lunches and snacks on their buses, so children would not go hungry while mobilizing a community of partners and volunteers (Peel & Muller, 2020).

INEQUITY—DIGITAL DIVIDE

With schools in all states having formal closure mandates and with forty-six of the states extending their original closure dates, education as it was traditionally delivered was disrupted. As of April 4, seventeen states had extended their mandated school closures through the rest of the academic year (Nagel, 2020); preparing schools to move to totally online instruction has required a massive undertaking and restructuring. The significant logistic considerations necessitated both planning and training (Einhorn, 2020).

As schools moved to an online format, digital inequities become more evident. School districts experienced difficulty providing the same online education to every student when some learners are not able to log on to the resources provided. Children who do not have access to a computer or families where a single computer is shared by multiple siblings or family members are at a disadvantage. In many cases, the less affluent or digitally savvy families are, the more their students are left behind because of the costs associated with digital devices and Internet access (Tam & El-Azar, 2020). Children without access to the Internet at home previously could use libraries, community centers, and restaurants to access Wi-Fi, but because of the COVID-19 pandemic closures, they no longer have access to these sources. Wooley et al. (2020) reported that according to the 2019 Federal Communication Commission report around 21 million individuals in the United States do not have access to broadband Internet at home. However, John Kahan, Microsoft chief data analytics officer, reported that his company's data indicated a more widespread problem. They estimate that almost 163 million individuals did not have access to broadband Internet speeds.

In an attempt to address this issue, many school districts across the country distributed digital devices and Wi-Fi hotspots to those students without the resources or ability to access online instruction during this crisis (St. George et al., 2020). For example, Jefferson City Public Schools in Louisville, Kentucky, distributed 25,000 Chromebooks to students without digital devices. New York City Schools estimated that they had 300,000 students without access to digital devices. They announced plans to lend iPads with T-Mobile connections; however, they found they only had 25,000 devices on hand, which raised concerns about those students who were not provided access to the needed instructional materials (Wooley et al., 2020).

For those students who remained digitally challenged, public television stations in some parts of the United States, including Los Angeles, New York, Detroit, Houston, Boston, Oklahoma, and Florida, just to name a few, are attempting to fill the gap by providing families with school-related programming (Wooley et al., 2020). An example from Oklahoma is RSU Public TV, which is bringing three hours per day of classroom instruction to viewers across all twenty-two counties in northeastern Oklahoma. The station has partnered with Tulsa Public Schools and Sequoyah Public School to bring different lessons to students during this crisis enabling students in rural towns to continue their learning (Hughes, 2020).

IMPACT ON FAMILIES

Not every student had a parent or caregiver available to work with them each day. People had to adjust lives to be able to facilitate your child's learning when that's not what you're used to doing (Einhorn, 2020). Having multiple school-age children in the same household complicated the process even further. These difficulties were compounded by children needing to use programs on a variety of platforms that require different logins and passwords that families now needed to master.

Although online learning content was being provided, the online approach did not work equally well for each learner. Those students with disabilities or who are English language learners were at more of a disadvantage than other learners. Additionally, school closures resulted in a widening of the achievement gap between low- and high-income students.

As the COVID-19 crisis continued more adults were out of work, thus increasing the number of students looking for work to support struggling families. This economic challenge impacted the options available to students upon graduation because of a lack of family resources that were allocated toward higher education (Wang, 2020).

FOOD INSECURE

Many students in the United States depended on meals they received through the National School Lunch Program that operated in nearly 100,000 public and nonprofit PK-12 schools. This program provides low-cost or free lunches to 29.7 million children daily. Free lunches were available to children living in households with incomes at or below 130 percent of the poverty level and reduced-price lunches to those children living in households between 130 and 183 percent of the poverty level. In 2018, nearly three-quarters of the 5 billion lunches served were free or reduced-price lunches (USDA, 2019).

For those students who were food insecure, schools instituted grab and go meals (McCarthy, 2020) because the federal government waived the requirement that meals be served and consumed in a congregate setting. This change in regulations was the result of an effort by the USDA to support social distancing (USDA, 2020). Although schools were closed, many school lunch employees continued to work so that they could provide free or reduced-price lunches to children in need.

Some districts also provided breakfasts for those children who are food insecure. These meals, which used to be available only during the school day, were available for families to pick up from their local school. Because of the dedication of these employees, children who are food insecure received meals (Pho, 2020).

GUIDANCE SERVICES

Students moving from high school to college faced the increased stress of having to grasp complicated financial aid packages and determine their anticipated out-of-pocket expenditures for higher education. School closures limited students' access to teachers, counselors, and other staff members who can support them as they attempt to make important decisions about their futures (Wang, 2020).

But those students transitioning from their K-12 experience to higher education were not the only ones experiencing stress. With schools being closed, students had limited access to contact with others outside of their immediate family. Educators realized the importance of facilitating student contact and are using social media platforms like FaceTime, WhatsApp, and Zoom to encourage students to communicate with their classmates (Reddy, 2020).

Many teachers used Zoom so that students could see and communicate with each other in order to help them stay emotionally healthy. Observing fifteen kindergarteners and their teacher on a Zoom call is a memorable experience! The students were so excited to see each other and had lots of experiences to share.

Students may express stress in many different ways. The Centers for Disease Control and Prevention (2020) indicated that stress can be exhibited through fear about one's own health or that of others, changes in eating patterns, difficulty sleeping or concentrating, or worsening of chronic or mental health conditions. School guidance counselors stepped in to try to fill this gap. The counselors made themselves available to support students during this crisis to answer students' questions, share ways to deal with stress, help establish new routines or keep up with regular routines, and be a role model for normal healthy functioning and social connections.

For example, Alachua County Schools, like many other school districts throughout the country, recognized the additional stress COVID-19 is placing on families and students. Families were able to contact school guidance counselors through phone or school email to set up appointments for phone or video chats (Alachua County Public Schools, 2020).

Reddy (2020) emphasized the importance of resilience and kindness when students are faced with the disruptions in their lives. These experiences, though difficult and trying, gave students an opportunity to develop their emotional resilience and become more adept as leaders.

INSTRUCTIONAL EXPERIENCE

Great shifts in academic content presentation occurred at unprecedented rates. One teacher reported, "In the last two weeks, I have had a lot of PD (both prescribed and personal) in order to be prepared for how we are delivering an online platform of learning through our Learning Management System, Canvas. All of a sudden, this training has become relevant and urgent." Another shared, "Our leaders are having to show grace and mercy to all stakeholders, including our employees." What is working for one right now might not be working for others. While one teacher may have a lot of technical training, there were others who only turn on their computer to take attendance and send an email.

Even with these enormous challenges, teachers made a difference for their students. One teacher shared, "Distance learning for my students is going well. We use a great communication tool called Class Dojo and 100% of my parents have the app so I can message them at any time. This app is something we have been using all year, but it is especially helpful right now during this crisis."

"I'm starting my students off slow and easy by having them complete an online lesson daily on iReady reading since they are familiar with it. I have been monitoring their daily progress and sending messages to them by providing 'feedback' on their quizzes. I'm requiring them to read independently daily and encouraging them to take AR tests after they finish the book they are reading. They are also getting math and science assignments from their content teachers and additional instruction from the art and music teachers."

TECHNOLOGY COMPANIES

To support students, education technology companies took drastic measures to help educators reach students in virtual ways. In many cases, the technology companies made their paid services free through the rest of the school year. In other instances, they lifted limits to services and/or added premium features to what is currently available free. Google, Microsoft Teams, and Zoom have remote learning tools that can be used by teachers to support teacher-created learning.

Companies offered prepackage content through programs such as iReady and Achieve 3000. Arizona State University is providing free access to field trips, puzzles, videos, and maps. BookCreator is supporting individual and collaborative writing skills by providing a free ninety-day upgrade to its premium service. Second language support is being provided by Carnegie Learning iCulture and Babbel (Schaffhauser, 2020). These are just a few of the many resources offered by technology companies.

IMPLICATIONS MOVING FORWARD

Although issues, strategies, and concerns changed constantly during the COVID pandemic, educators, resource personal, educational technology companies, and a myriad of other volunteers and employees worked long hours attempting to meet the needs of all students. As information about the crisis changed, educational leaders had to frequently adjust variables for adults and students in the school community. Educators' positive perspectives exemplified the actions and important difference they are making for K-12 learners.

LEADERSHIP IMPLICATIONS

Based on many topics discussed in this chapter, educational leaders needed to consider many attributes in providing educational services to children, training and support materials for teachers and parents, and communicate everchanging plans to all stakeholders. Managing tasks is the responsibility of leaders in any organization. The disruption to students, faculty, staff, and families during a crisis requires diligence in multitasking, communications, and actions.

DIGITAL CONCERNS

Understanding the realities, practicalities, and challenges students faced when working with technology was a leadership challenge. After deciding to deliver content online, the next major decision school district leaders faced dealt with how to deliver instructional content.

Students have significant experience using social media, but they are not as familiar with computer-based educational programs. Unlike social networking and other entertainment tools that are peer-driven and learned through usage, students are not likely to seek out, explore, and use educational technologies unless they are introduced to them and/or there is a need to use them for a useful purpose in a more structured setting (Ito et al., 2009). Consequently, with the rush to online instruction, educators were faced with teaching students ways to use educational technology while also trying to convey the academic content.

Moving a district from face-to-face to online instruction presented many challenges. The *New York Times* Editorial Board (2020) reported that in an attempt to provide online learning opportunities, about a third of the districts they interviewed were distributing digital devices to their students who needed them. Significantly fewer districts, however, were providing mobile phones or Wi-Fi hotspots to their students without connectivity. In fact, shortages of digital devices have forced many districts to ration laptops, tablets, and mobile hotspots (Lake & Dusseault, 2020). Some districts, such as Hillsborough County in Florida, limited distribution to one digital device per family, while other districts such as Anchorage Public Schools prioritized older students for receiving digital devices (Lake & Dusseault, 2020). New York City Schools faced the challenge of having only 25,000 devices available for 300,000 students (Wooley et al., 2020). The problem was not just finding devices but making sure that the devices could do what the students needed them to do (Lloyd, 2020).

Districts had to consider how to make distance learning accessible to all learners. Minneapolis Public Schools developed a distance learning plan that included guidance services for supporting IEPs, distribution of assistive technology, and measurement of progress for students with disabilities during this time of distance learning. The plan also outlined specific strategies for scaffolding learning for English language learners, homeless students, American Indian families, and other vulnerable or marginalized groups (Lake & Dusseault, 2020).

Palm Beach County, Florida, is another example of a district using technological resources for addressing student needs. The district announced it was continuing services for migrant students and classes for English language learners. General education teachers were responsible for accommodating students with disabilities, but special education teachers were available to answer family questions. IEP meetings continued but because of social distancing measures, they occurred over the phone or through digital platforms (Lake & Dusseault, 2020).

CHOOSING THE BEST METHOD

Challenges presented by a lack of digital devices were only one concern. With all instruction moving online, learners and their families were faced with having to choose the learning method that works most effectively for them. Those students who had access to a computer with an Internet connection could explore the options provided by their local district or could choose to enroll in a virtual school setting. For example, during the pandemic, Florida Virtual School increased its capacity so that it could serve 2.7 million students during the COVID-19 school closures. They prepared to handle ten times more students than they had served the previous academic year.

During the pandemic, this online school provided 100 free courses for K-12 students from general education courses to advanced placement (Dailey, 2020). Some students chose to move to a virtual school setting, but others for either social or academic reasons wanted to remain with their classmates and teachers.

CHALLENGES

Even if district leaders made the decision to place instruction online and the student chooses to stay with the district curriculum, there were additional challenges. The learning plan developed by the district often required parents who are already overwhelmed with attempting to balance working from home, possible unemployment challenges, difficulty meeting financial obligations, childcare issues, and multiple children for whom they needed to monitor and track academic progress, to provide the instructional support their students needed. During this pandemic, the Houston Independent School District's plan included project-based learning assignments for all students. Although there were plans for teachers' check-in calls, the plan was heavily dependent on student initiative and parental support to establish and maintain a daily routine (Lake & Dusseault, 2020).

If a district decided to put instruction online, the first question they needed to answer was what does digital learning mean to them? Districts chose to answer this in a variety of ways. Districts could decide to include prepared content, blended learning, flipped learning, personalized learning, or combinations of other strategies that used digital tools in varying degrees (Davis,

2020). As they prepared for the transition to online learning, no matter what components the district decided to include, they first needed to prepare the digital devices. This required significant time investment to make sure that operating systems, software programs, and security settings were appropriate for each device.

Then the districts needed to consider the learning management system (LMS) they were using. Some LMSs are free and some have costs involved. If a district had an LMS in place, they needed to consider if it could support the extra demands that would be placed on the system or use Canvas, Blackboard, or Google Classroom as their LMS, and each comes with its own unique challenges, especially for students and families who are not familiar with them.

A large investment of time was required to help educators, who have not depended solely on distance learning, understand how to operate securely and safely with children in a digital setting. But district administration and teachers were not the only ones dealing with this crisis. Technology specialists had to determine the appropriate security settings for each of the programs being used. But just as they figured these out, companies that had been attempting to solve the security problems changed their program settings. The software companies made changes, and then technology specialists needed to share the revised information with instructors (Lake, 2020).

Leaders had to act quickly in the spring of 2020 when schools closed their physical doors and made emergency plans to offer education virtually to students. As the months progressed, while originally unanticipated, the new school year of 2020–2021 required leaders to offer multiple options to students (virtually, face to face with modifications, or blended), based on the health situation in communities.

As data was presented from health officials, local decisions were made on the basis of safety concerns of students, staff and faculty, families, and communities. This required district leaders to prepare for multiple ways of instructing students through various mediums, training teachers to teach long term virtually or blended, and preparing building-based leaders to manage multiple delivery methods.

Most districts did not move to totally synchronous learning where teachers and students were engaged in live discussions. Instead, many used "asynchronous" or "hybrid" remote learning models incorporating instructional videos or daily assignments and feedback (Lake, 2020). Many districts began the remote learning process by providing enrichment materials, but as the required amount of time in distance learning grew, many moved from enrichment to instruction. For example, Governor J. B. Pritzker of Illinois extended school closures through the end of April and ordered school districts to transition to remote learning days rather than just enrichment days (Lake & Dusseault, 2020).

TEACHER TRAINING

Professional development was a significant concern since teachers are used to teaching in a face-to-face setting, not in the online setting. Two Utah Valley school districts explained their approach to this teacher preparation process. As they prepared to move instruction online, digital coaches set up simultaneous trainings in separate rooms spread throughout the district. The one digital coach in each room trained ten different schools at the same time on the learning platform, methods of assessment, video-recording options, and the software programs available. Then the small teams from each school went to their own school to train other teachers based on the training they had just received. As this process was enacted, the districts found that the coaches' stress level increased because they were trying to answer questions about programs and methods with which they were just becoming familiar (Lloyd, 2020).

As these teachers and coaches discovered, because of the variety of ed-tech tools available, it was important for the staff to know and understand the specific tools they were going to use online more thoroughly than they thought they needed to. This experience supports Gannon's (2019) findings that online instructors need to know the technology well enough to be able to troubleshoot for their students or themselves. The constant flow of here today and gone tomorrow apps and platforms makes it difficult for instructors to keep up with the tools that provide the most benefit for students. With the quick transition to online learning because of the pandemic, this knowledge-building could not occur (Gannon, 2019).

When preparing teachers to be online instructors, district leaders needed to determine if educators would be using prepared digital resources or whether teachers would be responsible for preparing their own content. If instructors were using software that the district had already purchased, such as iReady or Achieve 3000, these teachers needed training to familiarize themselves with how to operate, use, and track students' progress in the specific program. This would prepare them to troubleshoot for their students.

If the district administrators chose to have the teachers create the content, there were significantly more concerns. A thoughtful integration of technology that enables students to engage with their peers and enhance the learning experience (Davis, 2020) is the goal, but whether the speed of this transition during this panic-gogy allows for this is another issue. Shortly before the beginning of the pandemic, Schoology conducted a study called "The State of Digital Learning." The survey of 16,906 teachers and administrators, with nearly 97 percent of these from the United States, provided information about the state of digital integration in education. The majority of K-12 teachers and administrators who completed the survey agreed that technology positively impacted student growth and achievement. They also observed that online instruction can enhance learning experiences, save teachers' time, enable instructors to better tailor learning to student needs, aid in tracking student progress, and provide transparency in the learning process (Davis, 2020).

In teacher-created distance learning during this crisis, instructors needed training on the additional technical resources that can be used in their instruction. Videoconferencing platforms such as Zoom, GoToMeeting, Teams, and WebEx were used by educators to provide support and instruction to teachers as they transitioned to online instruction. These tools allowed for social distancing while providing visual contact and content sharing between participants, thus providing another venue for preparing teachers.

Software companies such as Boclips made videos available to teachers, which could be used to align instruction with standards. This program provided resources for helping teachers learn how to incorporate videos into their lessons. YouTube, the go-to source for many individuals, also provided short videos that could be used to familiarize teachers with many additional resources. However, having the time to explore and develop an understanding of tools during this crisis was a luxury.

Some districts made the decision to treat the online instruction occurring during this pandemic as a portion of the student's grade. This decision raised concerns about how assessment would be conducted. Some districts chose to use software such as Proctorio, a Google Chrome extension that monitors students taking exams online, in an attempt to create a more secure environment for assessment.

TIPS FOR TEACHERS MOVING ONLINE

Putting a course online requires more than just taking the face-to-face content and posting it online. In fact, Concieção (2006) noted that research participants indicated there was "intense work involved in designing and delivering an online course" (p. 35) both before and during the course. This made the delivery of online instruction more time-consuming than face-to-face instruction.

Participants indicated they perceived that more time was required for many aspects of online instruction. The instructional time in face-to-face and online instruction was approximately equivalent; however, grading and email communication time in online instruction were significantly greater than in the face-to-face setting. Another concern was that the grading time was increased because of a "lack of a computerized grading process in the distance course" (p. 110). This greater time commitment is an issue of which teachers should be aware. Tomei (2006) found that providing instruction through discussions, email, and chat increased time demands of the online course by a minimum of 14 percent over instruction in face-to-face courses. Van de Vord and Pogue (2012) determined that online instructors spent three times more time than face-to-face instructors just in the grading component of the online course.

In addition to time concerns, as an online instructor, it is particularly important to carefully consider the tone and the substance of written communication. In a digital environment, the lack of vocal inflections, hand gestures, and facial expressions can cause information to be received by students in a totally different light. For example, it is much easier to guide a student to a more skillful or accurate response in person than it is to accomplish the same feat through written feedback where even carefully phrased comments can be perceived as harsh or impersonal.

Creating good discussions, incorporating blogging platforms, and curating appropriate materials to accompany the course, all require a significant time investment. This course construction requires a totally different process than simply compiling your lecture notes from a chapter of the textbook (Gannon, 2019).

Gewin (2020) provided five tips for teachers as they moved their instruction online. The first tip focused on the use of videos. Videos are a great way to supplement instruction. They help to provide both visual and auditory support to further clarify the content. But it is important for instructors not to try to convert the entire lecture into a video.

Because of limited attention spans and learners' inability to remember too much content at once, video portions should not exceed thirty minutes. A series of short videos broken into sections makes the content more memorable and is also easier for students to replay if they become confused.

Instructors discovered that creating a video takes a long time. Generally, even if the instructor is familiar with the tools, creating videos requires three times as much work as a traditional lecture. No matter how videos are presented within the course, it is important to make sure that captioning or transcripts are included to comply with the Americans with Disabilities Act (Gannon, 2019).

It is essential to increase student engagement by encouraging student participation through feedback and peer discussions. As an instructor, identifying good digital tools that afford students with a substantive way of interacting with the instructor and other learners while engaging deeply with the course materials or applications. Tools such as Hypothes.is, a web annotation tool, or Padlet, which enables collaborative digit spaces, can enhance student discussions. Many LMSs include blog space features. However, if the LMS does not have one, using a tool like WordPress blog was helpful. When using digital tools, it is important to integrate these tools within the online content in a way that complements the pedagogical practices and accomplishes a specific learning goal. Choosing the appropriate tool for online instruction requires more than just identifying free or trendy tools. It requires a match between the content, learning goals, and the learners. The integration of all of these features required both time and a well-developed plan, which is what made the transition to online learning so difficult (Gannon, 2019).

Most important, teachers needed to check in with students often. Through student check-ins, teachers were able to identify students who were struggling or need additional support. Research has found that during the transition to online learning almost every student experiences some type of "performance penalty." This can become evidenced through lower grades than they earned previously, difficulty completing assignments on time, or even failure to complete the required assignments or courses. Those students who were struggling are particularly vulnerable to the performance penalty (Hart et al., 2017).

IMPLICATIONS MOVING FORWARD

During time of crisis, many learners experienced online learning for the first time. An online course can be a powerful learning experience helping learners become deeply engaged with the content. But this is not accomplished by chance. It is accomplished when instructors and students are present in the course and interacting with each other. This presence might be the single most important ingredient in making online learning meaningful. Research has found that presence needs to incorporate both a social and a cognitive feature. In the absence of either social or cognitive presence, online courses are no different from having a group of passive recipients crammed into an impersonal lecture hall. If this is the experience our learners received during the pandemic, they may have just as well viewed videos. As districts, technology specialists, and instructors work together we will be able to refine, expand, and improve on the instruction our students are receiving online.

LEADERSHIP MANAGEMENT

The massive transition from face-to-face instruction to online instruction took everyone by surprise. Technology, even with its many challenges and difficulties, invaded and took over education. There was no manual to support the transition or guidebook for providing the best possible transition (Lloyd, 2020). As teachers refined their skills in the area of distance education, the possibilities became more evident.

During this pandemic, providing instruction online through technology resulted in some unexpected issues. With virtually no social life outside of the work setting and having to work around families' computer usage schedules, teachers (like many other workers) found their workday expanding as they attempted to support every learner (Davis & Green, 2020). Educators need to identify and incorporate digital resources to provide the interaction needed in the online environment.

During this time of social distancing, we learned so much about the possibilities and the various ways and options available for distance learning. Whether technology and online learning have forever totally changed education, or whether it has only introduced more options, remains to be seen. During the pandemic, technology provided the social connections that everyone craved and provided a venue for continuing student learning, but what the future holds for educational technology and the role it will play in education is unknown.

Educational leaders were responsible for multiple tasks that required immediate changes in resource allocation, personnel assignments, training, and technology. Leadership personnel needed to be open-minded, empathetic, knowledgeable, and flexible, which are all attributes necessary for crisis leadership situations.

REFERENCES

Alachua County Public Schools. (2020). Coronavirus COVID-19. https://www.sbac.edu/Page/29814.

Center on Reinventing Public Education (CRPE). (2020). District responses to COVID-19 school closures. https://www.crpe.org/content/covid-19-school-closures.

Centers for Disease Control and Prevention. (2020, April 1). Stress and coping. https://www.cdc.gov/coronavirus/2019-ncov/daily-life-coping/managing-stress-anxiety.html.

Concieção, S. C. (2006). Faculty lived experiences in the online environment. *Adult Education Quarterly*, *5*, 26–45. https://www.researchgate.net/publication/286969150_Teaching_Time_Investment_Does_Online_Really_Take_More_Time_than_Face-to-Face.

Dailey, R. (2020, April 1). Florida Virtual School beefing up capacity to serve 2.7 million students amid COVID-19 closures. *WFSU News*. https://news.wfsu.org/post/florida-virtual-school-beefing-capacity-serve-27-million-students-amid-covid-19-closures.

Davis, L. (2020, February 6). Digital learning: What to know in 2020. *Schoology Exchange*. https://www.schoology.com/blog/digital-learning.

Davis, M. F., & Green, J. (2020, April 23). Three hours longer, the pandemic workday has obliterated work-life balance. *Bloomberg*. https://www.bloomberg.com/news/articles/2020-04-23/working-from-home-in-covid-era-means-three-more-hours-on-the-job.

Einhorn, E. (2020, March 16). As coronavirus closes schools, teachers and families brace for massive experiment in online education. *ABC News*. https://www.nbcnews.com/news/education/coronavirus-closes-schools-teachers-families-brace-massive-experiment-online-education-n1160966.

Gannon, K. (2019, March 25). 4 lessons from moving a face-to-face course online. *Chronicle Vitae*. https://chroniclevitae.com/news/2176-4-lessons-from-moving-a-face-to-face-course-online.

Gewin, V. (2020). Five tips for moving teaching online as COVID-19 takes hold. *Nature Career Feature*. https://www.nature.com/articles/d41586-020-00896-7.

Hart, C., Friedman, E., & Hill, M. (2017). Online course-taking and student outcomes in California community colleges. *Education Finance and Policy*, 13(1). https://www.mitpressjournals.org/doi/abs/10.1162/edfp_a_00218.

Hughes, H. (2020, April 7). RSU public TV launching on-air educational broadcast during COVID-19 crisis. *8 ABC Tulsa*. https://ktul.com/news/local/rsu-public-tv-launching-on-air-educational-broadcast-during-COVID-19-crisis.

Ito, M., Horst, H. A., Bittanti, M., Stephenson, B. H., Lange, P. G., Pascoe, C., & Mahendran, D. (2009). *Living and learning with new media: Summary of findings from the Digital Youth Project*. MIT Press.

Kamenetz, A. (2020, March 19). Panic-gogy: Teaching online classes during the coronavirus pandemic. *NPR*. https://www.npr.org/2020/03/19/817885991/panic-gogy-teaching-online-classes-during-the-coronavirus-pandemic.

Kandola, A. (2020, March 17). Coronavirus cause: Origin and how it spreads. *Medial News Today*. https://www.medicalnewstoday.com/articles/coronavirus-causes.

Lake, R. (2020, March 28). The latest from a nationwide survey: Districts continue to struggle toward online learning. *The Lens*. https://www.crpe.org/thelens/latest-nationwide-survey-districts-continue-struggle-toward-online-learning.

Lake, R., & Dusseault, B. (2020, April 3). School systems make a slow transition from the classroom to the cloud. *The Lens*. https://www.crpe.org/thelens/school-systems-make-slow-transition-classroom-cloud.

Lloyd, J. (2020, April 14). Utah Valley school districts proud of technology successes after COVID-19 forces dramatic changes. *Daily Herald*. https://www.heraldextra.com/news/local/education/precollegiate/utah-valley-school-districts-proud-of-technology-successes-after-covid-19-forced-dramatic-changes/article_a968c2d5-af4b-5e6b-b961-a38cf562632a.html.

McCarthy, K. (2020, March 6). The global impact of coronavirus on education. *ABC News*. https://abcnews.go.com/International/global-impact-coronavirus-education/story?id=69411738.

Nagel, D. (2020, April 9). Updated list of statewide school closures with closure dates. *THE Journal*. https://thejournal.com/Articles/2020/03/17/List-of-States-Shutting-Down-All-Their-Schools-Grows-to-36.aspx.

New York Times Editorial Board. (2020, April 6). The teachers union ate my homework. *Wall Street Journal*. https://www.wsj.com/articles/the-teachers-union-ate-my-homework-11586214731.

Peel, C., & Muller, B. (2020, March 18). Duval public schools to launch new home education program while campuses remain closed. *News 4 Jax*. https://www.news4jax.com/news/local/2020/03/17/duval-county-school-leaders-looking-at-options-for-online-classes/.

Pho, B. (2020, March 17). Grocers, food banks, and school lunch programs gear up to ensure residents have plenty of food. *Voice of OC*. https://voiceofoc.org/2020/03/

grocers-food-banks-and-school-lunch-programs-gear-up-to-ensure-residents-have-plenty-of-food/.

Reddy, J. (2020, March 19). Faculty, staff address student concerns for coping with COVID-19 stigma and stress. *The Cavalier Daily*. https://www.cavalierdaily.com/article/2020/03/faculty-staff-address-student-concerns-for-coping-with-COVID-19-stigma-and-stress.

Schaffhauser, D. (2020, April 10). Updated: Free resources for schools during COVID-19 outbreak. *THE Journal*. https://thejournal.com/Articles/2020/03/13/Free-Resources-Ed-Tech-Companies-Step-Up-During-Coronavirus-Outbreak.aspx?Page=1.

St. George, D., Natanson, H., Stein, P., & Lumpkin, L. (2020, March 22). Schools are shut, so how will kids learn amid the COVID-19 pandemic? *The Washington Post*. https://www.washingtonpost.com/local/education/schools-are-shut-so-how-will-kids-learn-amid-the-COVID-19-pandemic/2020/03/22/dac4742e-6ab7-11ea-9923-57073adce27c_story.html.

Tam, G., & El-Azar, D. (2020, March 13). 3 Ways the coronavirus pandemic could reshape education. *World Economic Forum*. https://www.weforum.org/agenda/2020/03/3-ways-coronavirus-is-reshaping-education-and-what-changes-might-be-here-to-stay/.

Tomei, L. A. (2006). The impact of online teaching on faculty load: Computing the ideal class size for online courses. *Journal of Technology and Teacher Education*, *14*(3), 531–41.

UNESCO. (2020, April 4). COVID-19 educational disruption and response. Author. https://en.unesco.org/covid19/educationresponse.

U.S. Department of Agriculture (USDA). (2019, August 20). National School Lunch Program. https://www.ers.usda.gov/topics/food-nutrition-assistance/child-nutrition-programs/national-school-lunch-program/.

U.S. Department of Agriculture (USDA). (2020). Nutrition program meal service during novel coronavirus outbreaks: Q & As. https://schoolnutrition.org/uploadedFiles/5_Learning_Center/13_Emergency_Planning/USDA-Child-Nutrtion-Program-Meal-Service-During-COVID-19-Outbreaks.pdf.

Van de Vord, R., & Pogue, K. (2012, May). Teaching time investment: Does online really take more time than face-to-face? *International Review of Research in Open and Distance Learning*, *13*(3), 132–46. https://www.researchgate.net/publication/286969150_Teaching_Time_Investment_Does_Online_Really_Take_More_Time_than_Face-to-Face.

Wang, J. (2020, March 20). How coronavirus could impact futures of students entering high school, college. *UChicago News*. https://news.uchicago.edu/story/how-coronavirus-could-impact-futures-students-entering-high-school-college.

Wooley, S., Sattiraju, N., & Mortiz, S. (2020, March 26). U.S. schools trying to teach online highlight a digital divide. *Bloomberg*. https://www.bloomberg.com/news/articles/2020-03-26/COVID-19-school-closures-reveal-disparity-in-access-to-internet.

Chapter 4

Remote Learning: Lessons in Social Awareness and Transformative Action

Keya Mukherjee

As discussed in the last chapter, leaders of all organizations have to make changes during times of crisis management. Educational leaders had to adjust to quickly changing facts that impacted students and learning, as evident by the COVID pandemic that began in March 2020 in the United States.

According to Li and Lalani (2020), globally, over 1.2 billion children were out of the classroom. School closures caused teachers to drastically shift their teaching from their familiar face-to-face format to online teaching. They were required to modify their instructional strategies and classroom routines quickly so that they could continue delivering instruction remotely on digital platforms. While learning online is popular and is often a preferred norm in higher education, while virtual school is a choice for many in K-12, and while many states require that an online course be a high school graduation requirement, pandemic school closures shifted teaching and learning for all students to an online format, with very little choice to access school-based support that many students needed.

Teaching online requires time to prepare, train in the new modality, become knowledgeable about e-learning tools to build online classes, and make shifts to work and home routines; however, in the quick transition to online learning during COVID-19 closures, school leaders and teachers had to make quick arrangements for the sudden shift away from the brick-and-mortar classroom and adopt online learning. There was little time to train or put well-designed learning materials online.

Additionally, school personnel became acutely aware that one of the big barriers to sustain remote learning during the closure was not only the lack of digital devices at homes but also the lack of digital access, such as computers, laptops, or tablets, but many homes did not have access to the Internet.

Many of these families had enough data to support cell phone coverage, but they had no access to broadband connectivity, which was required for online learning as they lived in remote, rural locations, or faced the prohibitive cost for telecommunication.

Many parents did not have the skills to support and engage their children in the new learning modalities, or manage multiple children on limited devices, while having to manage their own work schedules. According to Herold (2020), the transition to remote learning for U.S. K-12 education revealed the huge disparities that existed with basic digital access, and that these gaps in basic technology access were particularly stark along socioeconomic lines.

STRATEGIES

Instructional leaders investigated the topic of digital inequity that they were experiencing in their schools with the transition to remote learning using the Photovoice research methodology. This enabled a successful bridge to a virtual learning environment.

WHAT IS PHOTOVOICE?

Photovoice is a community-based participatory research (CBPR) methodology that puts cameras directly in the hands of the participants within a community, so they can explore and identify issues that are important to its members and share their lived experience with the issues. These findings from within the community enable researchers to gain a greater understanding of the issue(s) that people see central to their lives and employ social transformative action (Nykiforuk et al., 2011). The methodology was developed by Wang and Burris (1994) drawing from the theoretical foundations for critical consciousness, feminist theory, and documentary photography that uses the power of the camera to document social issues.

THE PHOTOVOICE PATH

Based on the work of Wang and others, Lorenz's (2005) Photovoice Path (figure 4.1) lays a journey for the CBPR that begins with identifying a topic within the community; learning about visual research; taking responsible photographs that represent experiences, thoughts, and feelings; discussing the photos with the participants; building story captions; and developing a dissemination plan to inform and encourage policy change (Lorenz, 2005).

A Photovoice Path

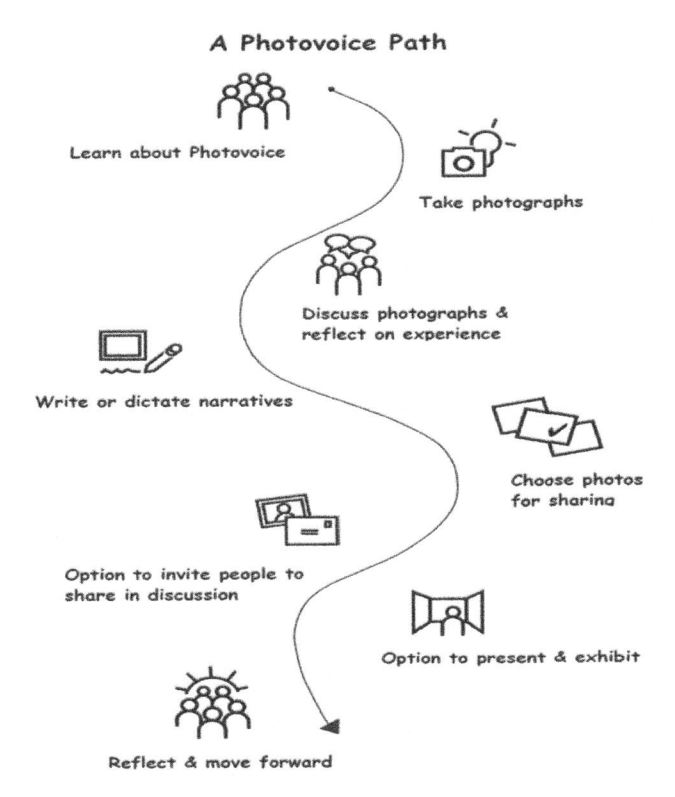

- Learn about Photovoice
- Take photographs
- Discuss photographs & reflect on experience
- Write or dictate narratives
- Choose photos for sharing
- Option to invite people to share in discussion
- Option to present & exhibit
- Reflect & move forward

Figure 4.1. The Photovoice Path
Source: Lorenz (2005)

USE OF PHOTOVOICE TO STUDY REMOTE LEARNING DURING CRISIS

Consistent with Photovoice methodology and the premise of student engagement, a modified version of Photovoice (Wang & Burris, 1997) was introduced as a qualitative research methodology for an action research project to instructional leaders, who are doctoral students in an eight-week graduate online course. For these school leaders, as researchers, the goal was to engage with CBPR and use the qualitative data to explore the lived experiences of diverse learners in their school community to develop critical consciousness and understand implications of social justice in the school community, as well as engage in transformative action.

The sudden closing of schools during the COVID-19 pandemic crisis and the quick transition to online learning allowed the course project to be realigned to the use of Photovoice to examine the challenges that families, students, and teachers were facing while engaging in distance learning.

Overall the Photovoice Path (Lorenz, 2005) guided the action research projects. Photovoice was introduced through a variety of readings, videos, and addressed during synchronous online sessions. Fifteen students became researchers, who started their Photovoice project path with a short concept paper exploring their topic with four preparatory questions:

1. How could you incorporate Photovoice to learn about diversity at your school?
2. What have you observed at your school that would want to learn about diverse students and issues that affect them?
3. What guiding questions do you have to frame your query or your interest?
4. Who would you like to have as participants from whose point of view you might want to study diversity at your school? Who could be involved?

These questions were modified to address the change in focus to issues of digital inequity, the challenges that families, students, and teachers were facing while engaging with distance learning at their schools. Revised questions included issues related to students from poverty, students with disabilities, support for students and families with distance learning, and instructional support for the learners:

1. How will needs of students who are unable to access digital platforms be met? How will the schools in the community provide academic instructional support while the schools are closed due to COVID-19?
2. How does distance learning affect students from a Title I school? What barriers exist for students in poverty to access online distance learning?
3. How is digital learning affecting the learning experience of students with disabilities?
4. What supports do families require to be successful with distance learning? How can parent and community involvement help support distance learning?
5. How do my students' home learning environments contribute to their success in distance learning? How do these home situations prohibit students from being successful in distance learning? What approaches best assist students transition during the homeschooling process?
6. What interventions can be implemented through digital platforms to support individual students? Who will provide these interventions and monitor the progress?

As schools shifted to remote learning, although gathering participants for the project seemed initially challenging, all the students were able to gather between one and two students and their families, or other stakeholders, from their school community to be part of the project. Communication between the researcher and participants was done via Zoom or by cell phone. With all the necessary permission in place, conversations about responsible photographing were discussed with the participants since the photos were to capture lived experiences with remote learning. Based on research ethics, elimination of any identifiable features of the children, the home, or the school was additionally emphasized.

An online discussion blog was set up to within the course to serve as a space to post critical reflections on the discussions being derived from conversations between the researcher and the participant on the purpose, meaning, and importance of each photo shared by a participant. The photo discussions were based on the SHOWeD methodology developed by Wang and Burris (1997), which comprises the following questions: What do you see here? What is really happening here? How does this relate to our lives? Why does this problem, concern, or strength exist? What can we do about it? Students created written discussions for each photograph based on conversations with their participants and shared these writings in the online discussion forum for a deeper and reflective conversation with peers. The photographs allowed them to see the daily lived experiences that were unfolding about the inequities of digital access and the challenges of remote learning.

For three consecutive weeks, students posted at least one photograph with the accompanying SHOWeD narrative. Figures 4.2 and 4.3 are two examples of work that the students did with the SHOWeD process and which was shared in the online discussion. Each week during group discussions, participants described and analyzed the photographs and expanding on the ideas shared by other students. The robust discussion during three weeks gave school leaders valuable insights into digital inequity and highlighted social justice with the imminent need for transformative action. They were able to identify themes, caption photographs, and prepare the data for sharing with stakeholders as the school year moved forward.

Themes that emerged from the students' projects included inequity with equipment as well as lack of Internet access, creating a home learning environment that would be conducive to remote learning, and lack of teacher preparedness to work with students with disabilities who lack student engagement during online learning, as well as supporting learning while supporting the needs of students in poverty.

> **S: What do you See here?** The student has drawn all over the board instead of completing the assigned activity.
> **H: What is really happening here?** The student was provided morning work prior to a live lesson. The student didn't listen to or does not understand the directions for the activity. The student became frustrated or bored and began to scribble.
> **O: How does this story relate to our lives?** The photo makes me feel sad and disappointed that the student was not engaged at this time. A lack of engagement will negatively affect the student's learning experience and content retention.
> **W: Why does this problem exist?** The issue could have come from many places. The directions may not have been given clearly or repeated. The student may have felt tired or uninterested in the activity. The student's activity should be continuously monitored during live lessons to better understand the issue.
> **D: What can we do about it?** To eliminate the issue, we must first understand it. Then provide a solution by either repeating directions, providing more frequent breaks, or choosing more engaging and relatable content, depending on the source of the issue.

Figure 4.2. SHOWeD1

Inequity with Equipment and Devices

Herold (2020) reported from a March 2020 survey of school leaders that lack of basic technology was a major problem in districts where there were high percentages of students from low-income families. Findings from the Photovoice project resonated with Herold's (2020) survey about lack of technology being a major problem within many school communities. In response to the crisis, based on the digital needs of the families, school districts provided a variety of resources to accommodate this difficult and unprecedented problem. Those who had digital access, but didn't have devices, received laptops or Chromebooks, so they were could web-based resources for their virtual classes; others without Internet accessed School on TV through the regional collaboration with a satellite network, but for the large number of students who were not digitally connected, course packets and workbooks

Remote Learning: Lessons in Social Awareness and Transformative Action 57

S: What do you See here? A mother parked in her van at a McDonald's parking lot connecting to internet on the first day of Virtual Learning. There are 5 children under the age of 7 in the van.
H: What is really Happening here? A determined mother is using her resources to support her child's education.
O: How does this relate to Our lives?
This photo shows a positive and a negative. The mother's willingness to find internet so her son can complete his assignments is a positive. The barriers low-income families face due to lack of resources is the negative.
W: Why does this situation Exist?
Schools were forced to shut down because of Covid-19. In an effort to continue educating students, Pasco County launched distance learning on Tuesday.
D: What can we Do about it? Although internet providers are offering free internet, several of the parents from my school live in remote areas where internet is not accessible. School staff is trying to find hotspots for impacted families.

Figure 4.3. SHOWeD2

were distributed for their weekly work. One school district identified in the group distributed hotspots to high school students who needed Internet access for their courses. Figure 4.4 captures this inequity that was shared during SHOWeD discussions.

CREATING A HOME ENVIRONMENT CONDUCIVE TO REMOTE LEARNING

Apart from technology, an important aspect of remote learning was parental involvement in creating a home environment that was conducive to support learning. A key observation from the Photovoice data showed that in the absence of structured classroom settings, students were learning in different parts of their homes, on different devices, amidst many distractions, and in environments that teachers typically deem are not conducive to learning. It was also observed that not all learning styles lend well to independent

Figure 4.4. Managing inequity with devices and access during remote learning

learning, particularly for students with learning disabilities, with language barriers, or other special needs that require small groups, one-on-one instruction, or remediation in foundational skills.

While some parents were able to provide the learning support needed for children to succeed with online learning, many parents had work schedules that kept them away from home during times when children were accessing online learning, or they did not have enough digital literacy to help children with gadgets on different platforms. With lack of support from parents, many children resorted to teaching themselves, and older siblings helped teach younger siblings.

In the quick transition to online learning, since teachers had the freedom to choose their online teaching schedule and platform, it was challenging for parents, who were balancing work and home, to maintain a schedule to support online navigation during live sessions for children in different grades on different platforms. Many parents expressed frustration that they were not comfortable assisting their child with the learning strategies being taught as students no longer had access to the direct support that these teachers provided during face-to-face interactions in the classroom. An instructional leader from a Title I school reported how a significant amount of time was spent to support parents on how to navigate the different distance learning platforms. Figure 4.5 captures the lived experiences of remote learning home environments during SHOWeD discussions.

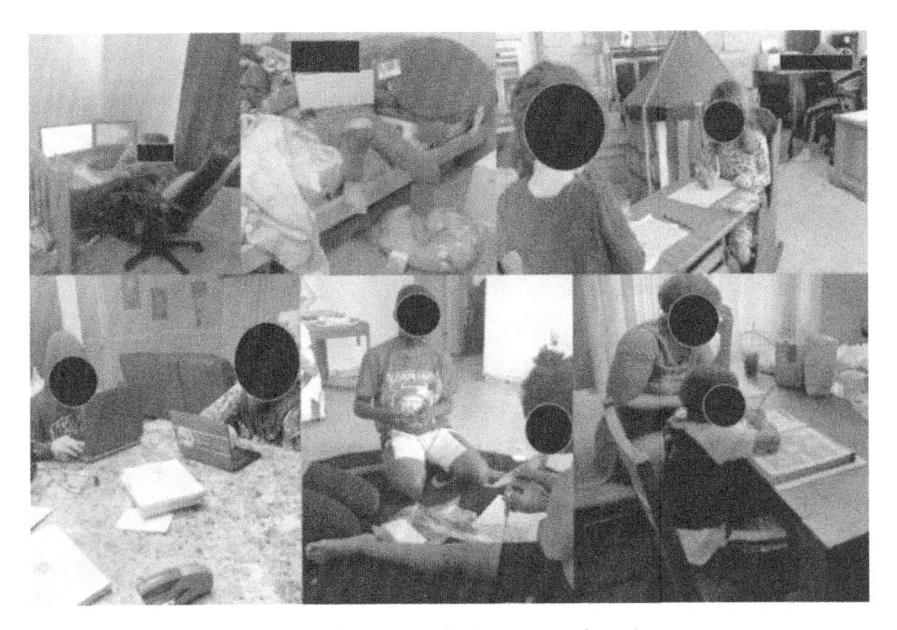

Figure 4.5. Home learning environments during remote learning

REMOTE LEARNING AND STUDENTS WITH DISABILITIES

As would be expected, Photovoice data revealed that remote learning was not conducive for students with disabilities because of the lack of support for these students to keep them engaged when learning. Research data from analyzing photos during the SHOWeD process revealed that often teachers did not have enough strategies to keep the student engaged, as learning modules were not structured to support independent learning. Additionally, multisensory instructions that are used as engagement strategies for students with disabilities (Graham et al., 2010) could not be provided for students during remote learning.

Photographs shared showed that students showed a pattern of inattentiveness and disengagement during their remote learning sessions. Without the necessary support, participants were often distracted and could not focus on lessons when attending live class time. One SHOWeD story shared the struggles of a parent trying to get a nonverbal child with autism to focus on the Zoom lesson, but without the adequate interventions in place the lesson couldn't be completed, as the child could not be engaged. Since students with disabilities need processes put in place to make learning happen during class, teachers had to become creative with artifacts from around the house to manage the student's attention during a remote session. A research participant

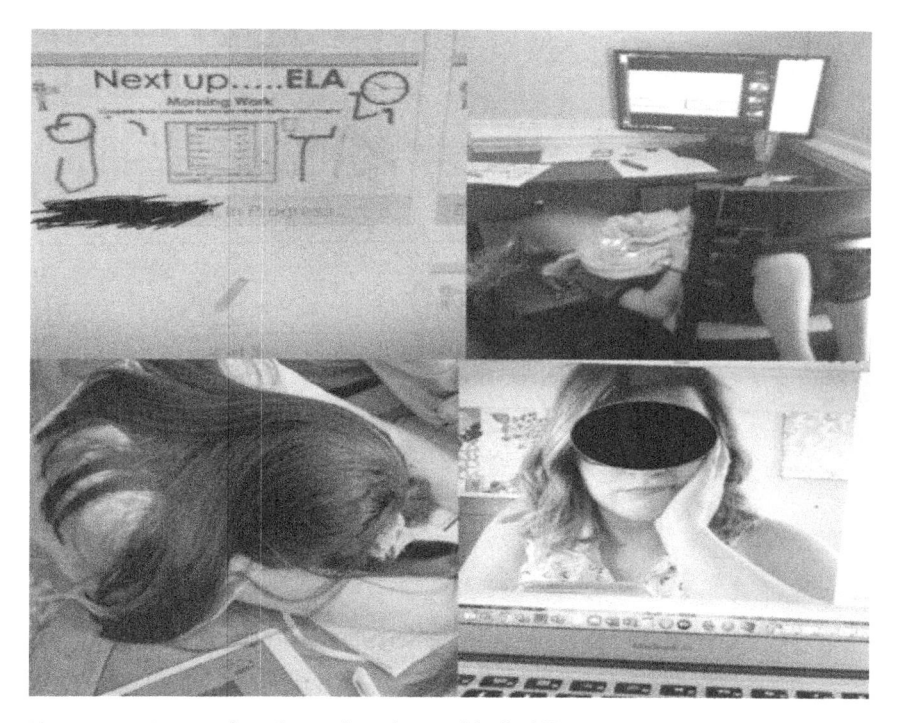

Figure 4.6. Remote learning and students with disabilities

working with students with exceptionalities reported that in times of uncertainty, such as with the pandemic, people with certain disabilities such as autism may express fears or frustrations with a simple change in environment from brick-and-mortar to online learning, so she warrants that if online learning had to continue during the following school year, there was a need to review IEPs to make sure that new needs are addressed to support students. Figure 4.6 captures these lived experiences of children with disabilities from SHOWeD discussions.

SUPPORTING STUDENTS IN POVERTY

The transition to remote learning was particularly difficult for those students in the lower-income communities, where Internet access was low to nonexistent. According to Fishbane and Tomer (2020), broadband adoption rates in low socioeconomic, particularly black and Latino, households are far below those in white homes, and that poorer the community, the less there was adoption of broadband connectivity. With remote learning, students from poverty, who were already vulnerable to falling behind, faced even more hurdles, as the support systems in their schools no longer existed.

Photovoice participants reported that while some homes had Internet access, others experienced delays with the Internet being set up, a resource they did not have prior to the pandemic. Once the Internet connection was established and a device checked out from the school, accessing learning resources and understanding curriculum expectations required continual support from the family and the teacher.

In high-poverty schools, purchasing and providing food and snacks, clothing, school supplies, and cleaning supplies for students (Teacher & Principal School Report, 2020) have high priority, as these basic supplies are a necessity for students to be prepared and ready to learn. Photographs analyzed from the Photovoice project showed that schools were looking for ways to reduce barriers for students of poverty and to supply students with food, clothing, and school supplies to ensure they were prepared for learning both on- and off-campus with the distance learning model that was put in place.

Remote learning from the pandemic had taken away the school's ability to provide the necessary resources, but with community support and caring stakeholders, schools provided food, technology devices, Internet, and school supplies to students in need. These items were picked up by family members or were delivered to the students' homes by teachers and staff. The goal was to reduce barriers and level the playing field for students in poverty.

The researchers observed that although distance learning continued to challenge students in poverty, positive efforts helped reduce barriers one at a time. The COVID-19 pandemic not only pointed the existence of digital inequity in low-income neighborhoods but also highlighted the inequity, which has always existed among those who live in poverty, with much needed basic resources, such as food and supplies that are needed to support learning.

Finding alternative instructional strategies when Internet was not available, such as Read-Alouds, was done over the phone; materials and resources, such as games and other activities, were provided for children to work at home with siblings or parents. Working with students required that teachers think creatively to deal with the new instructional demands that were placed on them as they juggled to handle different roles and deal with new stresses. Figure 4.7 captures the lived experiences of students in poverty from SHOWeD discussions.

Figure 4.7. Supporting students in poverty during remote learning

SOCIAL JUSTICE PERSPECTIVE BASED ON PHOTOVOICE RESEARCH WITH REMOTE LEARNING

Using Photovoice as a qualitative CBPR, the researchers, who are currently instructional leaders, got a close-up view into their students' home learning environment, one that they would not have had without the photographs and the ensuing conversations with the families. Full and equal participation of all students is the outcome of social justice in schools, so when groups of students are not able to fully or equally participate in distance learning, there is lack of social justice, which calls for transformative action.

The data on remote learning during COVID-19 raised awareness of the inequities of digital access, the struggles faced by students with disabilities, students in poverty, and the demands on parents' time as they juggled work, home, and children's remote learning environments, as well as teachers' struggles to adopt and adapt the new teaching modality. This awareness has helped build a vision of reform for bridging digital divide and building online education in a sustainable way by clearing the backlog and providing an environment that supports students and teachers.

LESSONS LEARNED AND TRANSFORMATIVE ACTION BASED ON PHOTOVOICE RESEARCH

Reflections at the end of a Photovoice project on remote learning during pandemic times showed an increased awareness for the barriers that occurred during the transition to distance learning. This awareness made it possible for instructional leaders to advocate and work toward future changes for a safe transition to the new school year. The Photovoice project enabled a group of researchers, who are school leaders, to not only generate new thoughts about inclusive leadership and transformative action, which included an understanding of digital access and literacy, renewed understanding of flexibility when dealing with students' adverse situations, an increased awareness of the struggles of students with disabilities and of students in poverty, but also use the gained understanding of their school community to support students and families.

A key observation from a school leader was about the use of Title I funds, that they can no longer be used as they have been in the past to provide for extra staff, extra supplies, and additional technology to economically disadvantaged students; instead, an additional consideration would be to use the funds to help students in their learning outside of school because it became evident that economically disadvantaged families need more support to learn at home with remote learning.

In looking forward, one researcher noted that while digital access was for all, it was particularly relevant and would be needed for students in poverty. Bridging the digital divide was therefore suggested as a high priority so that students could be equipped with devices and given access for remote learning ahead of time. Having a vision and a cohesive plan of action that considers a proactive approach instead of day-by-day survival was also recommended to handle online instruction and learning.

Based on data from the Photovoice study, another transformative change that was highlighted was a need to address how online education is delivered to students with disabilities. Researchers' experiences from the project showed that the current structure for online learning is not conducive for all students because of the lack of structures and processes that help them learn in a brick-and-mortar classroom. It is recommended that processes that help meets the needs of the learners by adjusting IEPs be put into place to make remote learning experience a more manageable endeavor for students with disabilities.

As school leaders during a pandemic, the researchers realized that preparedness included providing support to teachers who were overwhelmed with the change, since despite their lack of preparedness to perform the new duties, they were expected to move forward with grace and compassion. Commitment to remote learning required additional time to prepare lessons and monitor student participation (Karam et al., 2014). Participant teachers reported that although content was provided by district supervisors, teachers struggled with putting the content online in ways that would meet learning outcomes and support parents who had become partners in the learning process.

Dealing with parental struggles was also highlighted as an issue because many assignments required parental support, so parents had to spent a great amount of time helping children complete and submit assignments, which caused frustrations when parents did not have the skills or the knowledge or the time to support their children's learning. It was suggested that one way to manage this imbalance for both parents and teachers was to limit and vary the number of assignments that students were expected to complete and reshape current learning and grading procedures.

SUMMARY

Photovoice provided a group of school leaders the use of a tool to learn about current and pressing issues in their school community and to be able to lead during the unexpected and unprecedented crisis brought on by COVID-19. The in-class discussions, the reflective paper, and the Photovoice poster provided a structure for collaboration, reflection, and enhanced ways for the school leaders to generate new thoughts about inclusive leadership and transformative action, which included an understanding of digital access and literacy, renewed understanding of flexibility when dealing with students' adverse situations, and an increased awareness of the struggles of students with disabilities and those of students in poverty, but they also gained a deep understanding of how to support students and families to be able to adequately support remote learning. Being proactive as a leader is not just about preparedness with digital devices but also taking into consideration the barriers that families face and adapt accordingly.

REFERENCES

Ciolan, L., & Manasia, L. (2017). Reframing Photovoice to boost its potential for learning research. https://journals.sagepub.com/doi/pdf/10.1177/1609406917702909.

Dixson, M. D. (2015). Measuring student engagement in the online course: The online student engagement scale (OSE). *Online Learning, 19*(4), 1–15. doi:http://dx.doi.org/10.24059/olj.v19i4.561.

Fishbane, L., & Tomer, A. (2020). As classes move online during COVID-19, what are disconnected students to do? Retrieved from https://www.brookings.edu/blog/the-avenue/2020/03/20/as-classes-move-online-during-covid-19-what-are-disconnected-students-to-do/.

Gourlay, L. (2015). Student engagement and the tyranny of participation. *Teaching in Higher Education, 20*(4), 402–11.

Graham, D., Benest, I., & Nicholl, P. (2010). Learning in an inclusive multi-modal environment. *Journal of Cases on Information Technology, 12*(3), 28–44. https://doi.org/10.4018/jcit.2010070102.

Herold, B. (2020). The disparities in remote learning under coronavirus (in charts). Retrieved from https://www.edweek.org/ew/articles/2020/04/10/the-disparities-in-remote-learning-under-coronavirus.html.

Karam, E. A., Clymer, S. R., Elias, C., & Calahan, C. (2014). Together face-to-face or alone at your own pace: Comparing traditional vs. blended learning formats in couple & family relationship coursework. *Journal of Instructional Psychology, 41*(1–4), 85–93.

Klem, A. M., & Connell, J. P. (2004). Relationships matter: Linking teacher support to student engagement and achievement. *Journal of School Health, 74,* 262–73.

Li, C., & Lalani, F. (2020). The COVID-19 pandemic has changed education forever. This is how. Retrieved from https://www.weforum.org/agenda/2020/04/coronavirus-education-global-covid19-online-digital-learning/.

Lichtey, L. (2013). Photovoice as a pedagogical tool in the community psychology classroom. *Journal of Prevention & Intervention in the Community, 41,* 89–96.

Lorenz, L. (2005). The Photovoice Path. Retrieved from http://www.lslorenz.com/papers/PhotoVoice%20path-LSLorenz.pdf.

Masika, R., & Jones, J. (2015). Building student belonging and engagement: Insights into higher education students' experiences of participating and learning together. *Teaching in Higher Education, 21*(2), 138–50. https://doi.org/10.1080/13562517.2015.1122585.

Mayfield-Johnson, S., & Butler, J. (2017). Moving from pictures to social action: An introduction to photovoice as a participatory action tool. *New Directions for Adult and Continuing Education, 154,* 49–59. https://doi.org/10.1002/ace.20230.

Nault Connors, J. D., Conley, M. J., & Lorenz, L. S. (2019). Use of photovoice to engage stakeholders in planning for patient-centered outcomes research. Retrieved from https://researchinvolvement.biomedcentral.com/track/pdf/10.1186/s40900-019-0166-y.

Nykiforuk, C. I. J., Vallianatos, H., & Nieuwendyk, L. M. (2011). Photovoice as a method for revealing community perceptions of the built and social environment. *International Journal of Qualitative Methods, 10*(2), 103–24. Retrieved from https://journals.sagepub.com/doi/10.1177/160940691101000201.

Teacher & Principal School Report. (2020). Educators' funding priorities & personal spending. *Scholastic.* https://www.scholastic.com/teacherprincipalreport/funding-priorities.htm.

Theoharis, G., & Scanlon, M. (Eds.). (2015). *Leadership for increasingly diverse schools.* Taylor & Francis.

Trowler, V. (2010). Student engagement literature review. Retrieved from https://pdfs.semanticscholar.org/6d0c/5f9444fc4e92cca76fe9f426bd107e837a9f.pdf?_ga=2.115356230.133272658.1590806782-1966947899.1587660553.

Vygotsky, L. S. (1978). *Mind in society: The development of higher psychological processes.* Harvard University Press.

Wang, C. (1999). Photovoice: A participatory action research strategy applied to women's health. Retrieved from https://joycebredesen.files.wordpress.com/2015/09/photovoice-a-participatory-action-research-strategy-applied-to-womens-health.pdf.

Wang, C., & Burris, M. (1994). Empowerment through photo novella: Portraits of participation. *Health Education Quarterly, 21*(2), 171–86.

Wang, C., & Burris, M. (1997). Photovoice: Concept, methodology, and use for participatory needs assessment. *Health Education and Behaviour, 24*, 369–87.

Wang, C., Cash, J., & Powers, L. (2000). Who knows the streets as well as the homeless? Promoting personal and community action through Photovoice. Retrieved from http://citeseerx.ist.psu.edu/viewdoc/download?doi=10.1.1.473.9535&rep=rep1&type=pdf.

Chapter 5

Crisis Leadership: Educating Students with Disabilities in Times of Change

Georgina Rivera-Singletary & Michael Bailey

In the United States, 7.1 million children ages three to twenty-one received services under IDEA and receive educational support in addition to classroom instruction to provide effective learning opportunities that mitigate their learning disabilities (National Center for Education Statistics, 2020). Out of those, 64 percent of students with disabilities spend at least 80 percent of their time in general education classrooms (National Center for Education Statistics, 2020). Consequently, meeting the needs of special education professionals and the students they serve dramatically changed and the scope of practice for special educators was undoubtedly transformed during the COVID-19 pandemic.

The information provided in this chapter identifies what can be done by schools and educational systems in times of crises. Alternative ways of meeting student needs and how leaders can facilitate changes required, yet still meet mandates, is an important consideration for leaders.

The Individuals with Disabilities Education Act's (IDEA's) mandate to provide a Free Appropriate Public Education (FAPE) to students with disabilities is both a legal requirement and a moral imperative. However, as many special education professionals and government leaders have expressed, IDEA was not designed for this unprecedented and abrupt transition to mass online learning. "Provisions (e.g., free appropriate public education [FAPE]) were enacted with the understanding that students would be educated in face-to-face school and classroom-based setting" (Stahl et al., n.d., para. 2). Consequently, approaches to providing FAPE broke from the status quo as students found themselves interacting with a blended learning environment from home, in many cases with no, or limited, support from their special education teacher (Stahl et al., n.d.).

School breaks are often viewed by teachers and students as an opportunity to put the books down, go on vacation, enjoy favorite activities, and celebrate educational accomplishments. Many students enjoy being away from school for short terms and cherish the time when they return to see their teachers and friends, as well as to engage in school activities and socialize with peers. In the spring of 2020, as many students geared up for their spring break, a pandemic of global proportions known as COVID-19 disrupted the routines and expectations that guide the academic year. The lives of the world changed in an instant as many of the things we take for granted suddenly became anything but certain. Schools, businesses, churches, recreation centers, and leisure activity spots began to close their doors. As the world tried to adjust to the challenges presented by the COVID-19 pandemic, teachers around the country also scrambled to adapt their instructional approaches in ways that would still provide educational opportunities for students who could no longer congregate in physical school buildings. Students receiving supplemental services and education programs necessary for their education success all halted and the facets of each were changed.

Although all students were affected, some of the students most impacted by the unexpected changes (remote learning) resulting from COVID-19 school closure were students with disabilities. Classrooms across the nation were empty and had to transition to a virtual environment.

Educational leaders were responsible for ensuring appropriate services are delivered to students with disabilities. Homes became the least restrictive environment (LRE) that IDEA mandates for students with disabilities as well as hubs of isolation and social distancing.

Placements with typically developing peers, to the maximum extent possible, is a guiding principle of instituting LRE; however, reaching this is based on the availability of general education classrooms in schools.

LRE was designed to provide students with disabilities experiences in the classroom with nondisabled peers, a paradigm that has become increasingly complicated in an online environment. Martin (2017) found:

> A more "standard" legal application would be that virtual programs are in fact highly restrictive, as they offer no opportunity for education physically alongside nondisabled peers, and likely afford little or no opportunity for casual social interaction, such as takes place in the cafeteria, halls, or school grounds. (p. 11)

Students learning at home cannot be guaranteed placement in their LRE because districts do not have control over space, environment, and interaction with other students. Unfortunately, educating children, a practice that has traditionally struggled with the concepts of homogeneity versus heterogeneity in instruction (Murray et al., 2004), has become a one-size-fits-all approach with a focus on ensuring technology and Internet access for all students to connect with their teachers with limited room to focus on IDEA requirements. Instead of focusing on instructional opportunities, a myriad of resources and an overwhelming toolbox of packaged curricula that challenge the creativity of even the most astute and innovative educator have become the focal point of teaching (Camera, 2020).

The lack of organization of resources complicated the situation, especially since educating students without disabilities was just as complex as working with students with disabilities. Individual education plans (IEPs) designed specifically to meet the students' unique learning needs were lost in this shuffle and accommodations and modifications individualized for each student were possibly unachievable or, at best, subtle through virtual support. The degree to which these approaches were feasible at home is yet to be understood, let alone redesigned to ensure the provision of FAPE.

FRAMEWORKS: DIFFERENTIATED INSTRUCTION, RTI/MTSS, AND UNIVERSAL DESIGN FOR LEARNING

At the best of times, meeting the varied and complex needs of all students can prove challenging from logistical and pedagogical perspectives. Daily, hundreds of decisions are made in schools to develop an instructional plan that meets the needs of all students. At the forefront of decisions are data related to high-stakes assessments and measures of academic achievement. Students who are struggling or performing below expectations are often the focal point of instructional planning; however, the result is often an inundation of remedial classes in lieu of electives and repetition of foundational concepts at the expense of authentic opportunities for practice and growth (Hamilton et al., 2009).

Frameworks such as differentiated instruction (DI), multitiered systems of support (MTSS), and universal design for learning (UDL) are some of the most notable approaches to bridging the achievement gap between the highest- and lowest-performing students while providing targeted supports that help students progress. These frameworks are an attempt at providing instruction that meets the needs of all students, especially students who are struggling and at risk for failure, regardless of their learning style. Promoting various tiers of intervention for academic, emotional, and behavioral support is necessary and accomplished by using MTSS as a coordinated effort in classrooms by teachers.

This requires a collaborative approach for success since multidisciplinary teams should act as the cornerstone of student supports (Hamilton et al., 2009; Lowery et al., 2017). DI provides students individualized opportunities for learning that pique their interest and align with their learning styles. This is done in an attempt to give students open access to approaches that support what they learn, how they learn it, and how they can present their knowledge while simultaneously maintaining a connection with the identified objectives of a given lesson.

Specifically, DI allows a teacher to design instruction that differentiates the content, process, products, or learning environment to collectively support learning for all students (Tomlinson, 2002). Similarly, UDL has as its purpose to implement instructional methods that provide opportunities for students to have a variety of modalities for representation, action, and expression (CAST, 2018). Collectively, MTSS, DI, and UDL strengthen the learning opportunities for all students while encouraging collaborative processes and teaming among professionals, especially those working on behalf of students with disabilities (Lowery et al., 2017).

During the crisis of COVID, leadership and management had to attempt to meet the requirements of IDEA. The absence of classroom space and one-to-one contact with students had increasingly challenged the provision of educational supports required by the IEP. Accommodations and modifications that are the backbone of education success for students with disabilities were altered or redesigned, especially concerning were those services required for students with physical disabilities (The Hunt Institute, 2020).

Special educators rely on coordination and collaboration to implement education frameworks that drive initiatives and decisions for educational success and these efforts have been reduced to telephone calls or virtual meetings. Consequently, instruction packets took the place of teacher-led instruction, blended with complicated platforms, and an occasional one-to-one conference with a teacher leading to massive confusion for educators and students alike. Limited opportunities for collaboration widened the gap between the practices of general education and special education teachers.

In addition, navigating a system that is intensely complicated, especially absent the supports typically provided by school staff, can be troublesome for many families, especially students and families from traditionally marginalized populations. Consequently, an already challenging education system replete with regulations and professional jargon for special education students rendered itself a web of tangled processes not fully understandable to families.

Even before the challenges presented by COVID-19, teachers struggled to reach all learners, thus marginalizing and excluding many students. Research showed that a strong teacher–student relationship helps mitigate at least some of these barriers due to increased opportunities for engagement based on a foundation of mutual respect and collaboration (Jensen, 2013). Since COVID-19, teachers lost their ability to connect with students personally, a crucial factor necessary to support basic student needs (e.g., food, shelter, safety nets).

Providing supports beyond academics that once were facilitated through school attendance was completely interrupted. Although many schools made admirable attempts at meeting the basic needs of students through initiatives such as curbside loading of nonperishable food into the trunks of family vehicles, there was a significant gap in providing the most basic supports that many students needed.

Because of school closures, the role of the teacher belonged to parents who, in many cases, relied on teachers to be the expert as it relates to educational issues. Unfortunately, the expertise of the teacher was also lost in the pandemic, as they too felt like novices navigating a virtual world they were not a part of prior to COVID-19.

Although there were parents who were able to rise to the education challenge, had the appropriate technology and connectivity to create effective "classrooms" in their homes, and had agency to change and adapt to the new normal, many others lacked some or all of the preconditions necessary to establish effective learning environments outside of the school building. Consequently, hegemonic structures that have promoted the success of some students while failing to support many others were reinforced as the gap between those with and without the ability to support the educational needs of children became increasingly apparent without the supports offered in the school building.

These issues, paired with families who lost their jobs and their ability to feed their children, had low levels of education, or could not understand the material being provided to their children, have greatly exacerbated the problems that were already prevalent in the education system. This created a necessity to reconsider both curricular and pedagogical structures in order to better meet the needs of students. As Antoninis (2020) noted, "We need new ideas to ensure education responses to COVID-19 don't harm those [who have been] marginalized" (para. 1).

The challenges of implementing special education services under the IDEA are numerous and well documented beyond the scope of this chapter (e.g., Davidson & Gooden, 2001; Friend, 2016; Reeves et al., 2010). However, one commonality among many of these problems is a pedagogical approach rooted in educational paradigms that have remained largely unchanged since the first public school was founded in the United States nearly 400 years ago.

Like the structures of a tree, wherein leaves give way to branches, which give way to a trunk, which in turn is supported by an organized structure of roots, the American educational system is predicated on a foundation of hierarchical arrangements (e.g., administrators overseeing teachers who, in turn, oversee students; unit learning goals leading to daily learning goals that lead to instructional activities, etc.).

These structures are multipurposed. They may serve as a way to help students build subsequent layers of knowledge through a common progression, as an administrative tool for the management of a complex institution, or as a roadmap to ensure a sense of instructional consistency among schools. Simultaneously, they are a reflection of the power structures of the broader society, structures that have traditionally served to marginalize certain groups while reinforcing the privilege of others (Deleuze & Guattari, 1988). As Hodgson and Standish (2009) noted:

> The tree is both metaphor and example. Dominant knowledge is not an abstract entity carried and transmitted in ideology but is grounded in institutions and ways of speaking, writing and representing. These in turn are based on deep-rooted and interlinked ways of thinking developed and further entrenched over centuries, the tree's branches providing the shelter of tradition. (p. 321)

Such structures are both symbolic representations of societal power dynamics as well as tangible edifices through which the execution of pedagogical practices are mediated.

If the 2020 COVID-19 pandemic taught us anything about educational practices, it is that the structures on which we have traditionally relied have proven inadequate in the current circumstances. Curriculum maps, state standards, and high-stakes assessment were necessarily set aside, and the creativity, determination, and professional skills of administrators, teachers, and school support staff became increasingly necessary aspects of instructional planning. In addition, students and their families became integral to the education process as active participants, rather than passive recipients of knowledge, demonstrating adaptability, resourcefulness, and grit as their role in the learning experience became more visible.

This focal shift is reminiscent of Deleuze and Guattari's (1988) metaphor reflecting the nature of botanical rhizomes. Deleuze and Guattari (1988) claimed, "Plants with roots or radicles may be rhizomorphic in other respects altogether . . . burrows are too, in all their functions of shelter, supply, movement, evasion, and breakout" (p. 7). Furthermore, "a rhizome has no beginning or end; it is always in the middle, between things, interbeing, intermezzo. The tree is filiation, but the rhizome is alliance" (Deleuze & Guattari, 1988, p. 27).

Rhizomatic approaches abandon the arboreal notion of hierarchical learning, instead embracing a sense of intentional nomadism. Through such a paradigm, educators can use broader goals and destinations to guide the learning experience while allowing students to engage with the learning process in ways that pique individual interests and learning styles (Cole & Korkmaz, 2013; Goodley, 2007). Such a philosophical approach is by no means new to the COVID-19 pandemic and can be seen in instructional methodologies such as UDL (Hitchcock et al., 2002) and learner-active, technology-infused classrooms (Sulla, 2018); however, the necessary adjustments that schools throughout the United States made in light of closures provide a timely opportunity to consider how we might approach pedagogy in ways that breakdown the extant structures that continue to underserve many of our most vulnerable students.

Although rhizomatic learning approaches can benefit each and every student, they are an especially powerful framework for supporting students who have traditionally been underserved by the arboreal structures of the education system. For students with disabilities, in particular, the nearly fifty years since the passage of the IDEA have resulted in significant improvements in access and services; however, educational outcomes for these students still fall short of those experienced by their nondisabled peers (Goodman et al., 2011; Rabren et al., 2002; Sullivan et al., 2014).

This may be, in part, due to the fact that the foundations on which the IDEA were built still rely on the structures that were ill-prepared to adequately serve students with disabilities prior to the IDEA's passage in 1974. Rather than supplementing such a system, students with disabilities may be more effectively served by a framework wherein

> the principles of the rhizome are plotted against the desired outcomes and the resultant cells get populated with a substantiation of the learner's performance in a particular field... [resulting in a] design [that] is not hierarchical, but rather a flat plane describing the points where the best connections for a particular learner occur. (Cronje, 2017, p. 16)

In doing so, teachers, students, and families became partners, actively pursuing the lines of flight through which authentic learning and flexible pedagogies connect to create spaces where the students' understanding can grow and stretch, reterritorializing the educational experience as students, ideas, and activities genuinely connect with one another in a student-focused learning paradigm. The following section will explore how this notion of rhizomatic learning can be actualized through a framework based on the principles of UDL and the requirements of IDEA.

When the Education of All Handicapped Children Act (1974) was introduced nearly fifty years ago, it promised to bring a greater level of equity in the educational opportunities available to children with disabilities. As the U.S. Department of Education (USDOE, 2010) document noted, "No belief is more damaging in education than the misperception that children with disabilities cannot really succeed and shouldn't be challenged to reach the same high standards as all children" (para. 4). To this end, the EAHCA, which later became IDEA, put forth the mission of ensuring all students receive "an education that prepares them to be full participants in our economy and our communities" (USDOE, 2010, para. 1). Despite its many accomplishments,

IDEA has ultimately fallen short of these goals. This is, at least in part, a manifestation of the foundations upon which IDEA services are built.

Many children with disabilities experience the learning process in ways that may be different but are just as valid as those experienced by their peers. Different modalities of acquiring information, expressing knowledge, or interacting with the school environment can create very different needs when considering how to engage the learning process.

IDEA is predicated on the notion that, through the provision of services, related services, and accommodations, the individualized needs of learners can be bridged so that they can receive meaningful benefit from their educational experience. Although this is true for some learners, others still find themselves deprived of the benefits to which they are entitled, as evidenced by graduation rates (Pyle & Wexler, 2012) and post-school outcomes (Mazzotti et al., 2016) that point to significant shortcomings in the promises we have made to students with disabilities.

The limitations of IDEA are, in some ways, unsurprising. Despite its ambitious goals, IDEA is ultimately a new structure built on top of existing educational structures that historically excluded individuals with disabilities either through direct denial of education or relegation to other schools and settings until students eventually graduated or dropped out of school. Although IDEA can be thought of as an enhancement to the existing educational system, it has proven incapable of fundamentally changing the nature of our practices. Rather than shifting pedagogies, the extant structures have forced special education services to adapt to the general education paradigm.

IEP services are often delivered with a frequency that is administratively convenient and designed to provide "extra support" to some students, regardless of whether they need more or less at any particular time or with any particular content (La Salle et al., 2013). IEP goals are often cloned from IEP to IEP and from student to student (Christle & Yell, 2010), leaving minimal individualization. In the end, special education services fail students because the general education structure on which such services are predicated is inherently flawed.

The failings of general education pedagogies became increasingly clear during school closures associated with crises that alter school schedules, personnel, and facilities. The COVID pandemic exemplified this. Leaders had to implement multiple changes for multiple stakeholders and students. Teachers who were suddenly thrust into unknown territory found themselves faced with the monumental task of creating new learning paradigms.

With little time to prepare, this new, fully virtual milieu often, especially in the early stages of implementation, fell back on the arboreal structures that education professionals have advocated abandoning over the past two decades, such as packets of worksheets, packaged curricula, and lecture-centric class meetings (Au, 2011; Demko, 2010). Similarly, special education services mirrored their traditional counterparts by holding virtual resource rooms, attending a percentage of scheduled class meetings, and continuing to hold annual IEP reviews wherein many IEPs were indistinguishable from their preclosure counterparts, despite drastically different needs for some students.

Guidance from the Office of Special Education and Rehabilitative Services (OSERS) (2020) was sparse, vague, and at times confusing, leaving educators with little else on which to fall back. Despite these challenges, there were many educators who willfully broke the mode, creating dynamic and innovative ways of connecting with students and engaging them in authentic learning. One approach for doing so can be found in a rhizomatic approach to UDL.

With roots in environmental accessibility, the concept of UDL offered educators an opportunity to reconceptualize concepts of equity and access for all students (Lowery et al., 2017; Smith Canter et al., 2017). UDL challenges us to consider the notion that, for many students, curricula and pedagogy are "disabling" factors rather than an innate deficit within an individual (Edyburn & Gardner, 2009). For example, in a building where a ramp and motion sensor door ensure that individuals with varied mobility needs can access the front door, we can consider that there is no "disability" (i.e., etymologically speaking there is no lack of ability); there is simply a diversity of mobility and modalities for interacting with the entrance.

Similarly, in the classroom, if all students are told that they must read the same novel from the same paperback copies of a book, there may be students who, despite being capable of understanding and discussing the topic, are unable to fully engage the curricula, not because of their abilities but because of structures that possess inherent assumptions of normativity. Instead, if students are given the opportunity to engage that same text with audiobooks, screen readers, digital copies, overlays, or any other number of tools, in addition to the paperback copy, all students, those with and without diagnosed disabilities, have the opportunity to interact with materials in ways that are most conducive to supporting their learning.

STRATEGIES THAT WORK

At its heart, UDL is a rhizomatic process. This fact can be seen in the three guiding principles undergirding UDL that advocate instructional methodologies based on multiple means of expression, representation, and engagement (CAST, 2018). Like traditional pedagogies, an educator begins the process of designing UDL-focused lessons through the development of learning targets;

however, the instructional paradigms otherwise diverge significantly. Rather than structuring a lesson that relies on students following set trajectories like a plane chartered from one airport to the next, UDL allows educators and learners to follow the natural progression of inquiry and exploration that promotes critical thinking and active engagement (Edyburn, 2010; Hall et al., 2012).

Such a process gives way to learning experiences "characterized by principles of connection, heterogeneity, multiplicity, asignifying rupture, cartography and decalcomania" (Hodgson & Standish, 2009, p. 322). This flexibility allows for natural exploration and learning environments that are flexible and responsive, meeting students when and how they most need. In the following section, we will explore how such a process may look in practice and how such rhizomatic archetypes can be used flexibly to support students with disabilities in brick-and-mortar classrooms, in virtual learning environments, and in unchartered territory such as during the COVID-19 closures, in hopes that we can begin to move beyond the arboreal edifices that have historically marginalized students with disabilities.

The absence of a structured and professionally designed lesson plan for students promotes an opportunity to develop a collaborative and contextual learning experience for students vis-à-vis rhizomatic learning principles. Embedded within these types of learning experiences are opportunities to engage with innovative cognitive, social, and teaching presences that challenge the status quo, yet promote an "eco-system" that stimulates a student's own understanding and knowledge-building abilities (Bozkurt et al., 2016). Three factors guide rhizomatic lesson development and provide the building blocks: learner-learner, learner-teacher, and learner-context, each working together to establish a community in which curriculum can be co-constructed (Cormier, 2008).

Students with disabilities should be allowed to move in and out of the varying spaces, both physical and metaphorical, they are occupying. Allowing them to wonder through a lesson and individualizing their meaning-making experiences in a virtual platform can perhaps be the most impactful to their individual learning style. Instead of allowing students to struggle as they navigate content and concepts that may not seem relevant to them as independent learners, making connections between previously learned concepts and other world encounters can prove fruitful to their personal and academic growth.

Rhizomatic learning is not fueled in a controlled or organized environment; rather, it is stimulated through an aggressive, chaotic, and resilient space (Bozkurt et al., 2016). Similar to the environments that many students with disabilities are currently occupying, a rhizomatic learning approach allows for students to engage in small group learning, to be active participants in large groups, and to access hands-on experiential activities that promote deep learning and generalization.

Although the status quo demands structured areas with fixed schedules, a rhizomatic approach delivers opportunities for a new type of learning and a reconsideration of delivery models special education services. Encouraging nomadic learning experiences unforeseen by students in a regular classroom can lead to a becoming and coming to understand opportunity wherein learning takes on a life of its own and students pave their own way to knowledge (Bozkurt et al., 2016). Although brick-and-mortar education classrooms are unattainable, rhizomatic learning posits that a creative space is ultimately what leads to a knowledge-building experience where students can thrive, and this can be anywhere.

The pandemic of COVID-19 contributed to a system of confusion, inequity, and seemingly unachievable educational opportunities. Consequently, the education system was thrust into a new world of being and doing. Embracing the new normal and opportunities to establish learning structures that attend to students in varying environments may ultimately be a gifted to educators. All is not lost as education is a blank slate in which creativity, innovation, and accessibility for all students can be achieved.

Rhizomatic approaches can support this new way of learning by providing the tools necessary for engagement and enticing students to enter their learning environments with endless possibilities. The precursor for this model of learning follows a learner-teacher, learner-learner, and learner-context modality of rhizomatic experiences that can "reterritorialize more open-ended alternatives" (Harris, 2016, p. 219).

LEARNER-TEACHER

In keeping with rhizomatic learning, teachers can take advantage of promoting unique uses of the tools as an individualized experience for students and families. For example, in the learner-teacher phase of rhizomatic learning, the teacher presents a concept through video or online tool with a blank slate, an empty and open space where the student and family can type or talk at the same time the concept is being presented.

Conversations related and unrelated to the topic ensue and eventually blend to form understanding for students. In the classroom, where side conversations can detract from teacher-centric lectures, the virtual environment allows for both engagement with direct instruction and simultaneous free thought, questioning, and dialogue in synchronous chat. Instead of disabling and policing comments, it is through this space that the students begin to simultaneously design a curriculum that makes sense to them in their own world and taps into their creative space (Bozkurt et al., 2016). Teachers can engage topics as they emerge and can use the lines of flight that organically surface to design subsequent activities.

LEARNER-LEARNER

Inclusive education inadvertently has become prevalent in the virtual classrooms that resulted from COVID-19 since all students are equal learners. Teachers provide lessons that are predeveloped, and students connect to with other learners. Learners with similar needs can be scheduled together to have interaction with the community of practice that the teacher has presented. The parent can be a part of this or other family members. Knowledge does not preexist among the group; rather, it is co-constructed through interaction and camaraderie because, in this space, knowledge is negotiated in collaborative and contextualized ways (Bozkurt et al., 2016).

LEARNER CONTEXT

Students build knowledge by making connections with other environments, nature, and contexts. In essence, they are building their own learning experiences without fear of struggling through predetermined activities that may not be accommodated in the current learning environment. This type of learning is a form of place-based education, which closely aligns with rhizomatic principles in that learning happens in all places (Bozkurt et al., 2016).

Place-based education constructs learning through the use of individual places or locations. "Learning in these moments is organic and visceral. There's much to learn from the places we inhabit—from traveling across the globe to getting out into our own communities" (Getting Smart et al., 2017, p. 1). When thinking about the nomadic way of how learners create learning paths in unexpected places, place-based learning can promote "student agency, boost access and opportunity, prioritize deeper learning and personalize learning" (Getting Smart et al., 2017, p. 4) aligning with rhizomatic principles of design to try, monitor, fail, reflect, rethink, redesign, and reiterate structures (Bozkurt et al., 2016).

LEADERSHIP STRATEGIES

As states and districts contemplated a return to brick-and-mortar schools during the fall of 2020, school leaders planned on implementing specific strategies in anticipation of the challenges new rules and regulations demanded. These changes extended far beyond the scope of the COVID-19 pandemic and a return to physical school buildings.

Administrators and teacher leaders were afforded an unprecedent opportunity, in the midst of adversity, to build cultures and structures that encourage more collaborative approaches to supporting students. Just as rhizomatic structures allow for an endless possibility of connections and deviations, school leaders can set the conditions by which teachers, students, and communities can work in tandem to follow lines of flight, deterritorializing curricular arrangements in ways that promote flexibility, engagement, and exploration. All of which require personal and organizational change and creativity.

One way that leaders can put such rhizomatic notions into practice is through a reimagining of the master schedule. As it stands, many school districts contemplated a variety of learning modalities ranging from traditional face-to-face instruction to fully remote learning, with a variety of hybrid models in between. By necessity, such models changed the ways in which schools conceptualize teacher planning, professional learning communities, and student schedules.

Rather than assuming that traditional scheduling models can be adapted to this new paradigm, leaders can reimagine instructional planning and delivery. One example of this would be to abandon the notion of the grade-level versus content-area "teams." Such structures have historically situated the knowledge of general education teachers as the cornerstone for curricular planning; however, this also discounts meaningful contributions of support staff such as special education teachers, school counselors, social workers, and a variety of other essential and valuable individuals.

These models isolate knowledge in a linear modality (e.g., all fifth-grade teachers pacing together; the entire math department planning units of instruction). Although this is not inherently deficient, it does not account for the benefits of varied groupings wherein cross-disciplinary, cross-grade, or cross-specialty staff can each contribute meaningfully to the construction of authentic learning opportunities in lieu of standardized instruction.

Another way that leaders can approach schoolwide supports from a rhizomatic perspective is through the provision of greater autonomy for noninstructional support staff such as paraprofessionals, academic coaches, office staff, and so on. As responsibilities necessarily adapt to the new normal in schools, these staff members have an opportunity to redefine roles and contributions.

For example, instead of acting as a monitor or minor role player in the classroom, a paraprofessional may focus more specifically on the supports necessary to provide students with disabilities equal access to their learning experiences. Rather than simply escorting their students to an elective and sitting in the back of the room or with a student who is having difficulties, the paraprofessional might act as a conduit, bridging cross-curricular concepts in environments that the classroom teacher might never get to experience.

Building this environment of creativity will filter down to students and promote opportunities of the nomadic way of learning that rhizomatic structures provide. Likewise, office support staff who may not be needed to act as the first point of contact in the school may take a more active role in engaging families and community partners in the educational experience, supporting connections to learning at school that may have evolved at home during remote learning. Such possibilities are endless and wholly adaptable to the needs of individual districts, schools, and students.

SUMMARY

COVID-19 crisis was a precipitating event that resulted in a convoluted maze of challenges in all facets of life. Consequently, navigating a "new normal" became the journey. From the classroom to the living room, education has not escaped the mass exodus that many faced during the pandemic. Absent in all is an effective plan to make the transition quickly, efficiently, and effectively. The latter continues to challenge efforts to mitigate the gaps in the educational processes. Amidst the vast number of "classrooms" resulting is an opportunity to revamp, revise, and creatively redesign education for students that puts the steering in their hands as they become their own navigators of knowledge.

REFERENCES

Antoninis, M. (2020, April 4). We need new ideas to ensure education responses to Covid-19 don't harm those marginalized. *Worlds of Education*. https://www.worldsofeducation.org/en/woe_homepage/woe_detail/16743/%E2%80%9Cwe-need-new-ideas-to-ensure-education-responses-to-Covid-19-don%E2%80%99t-harm-those-marginalized%E2%80%9D-by-manos-antoninis.

Au, W. (2011). Teaching under the new Taylorism: High-stakes testing and the standardization of the 21st century curriculum. *Journal of Curriculum Studies*, *43*(1), 25–45. https://doi.org/10.1080/00220272.2010.521261.

Bozkurt, A., Honechurch, S., Caines, A., Bali, M., Kourtopoulos, A., & Cormier, D. (2016). Community tracking in a CMOOC and nomadic learner behavior identification on a connectivist rhizomatic learning network. *Turkish Online Journal of Distance Education*, *17*(4), 4–30. https://pdfs.semanticscholar.org/0b11/325fef20fef146483bc4dfa71bee964ed4e8.pdf.

Camera, L. (2020, April 6). Education interrupted. *U.S. News & World Report*. https://www.usnews.com/news/education-news/articles/2020-04-06/teachers-prepare-for-lessons-after-lockdowns.

CAST. (2018). Universal Design for Learning Guidelines version 2.2. http://udlguidelines.cast.org.

Christle, C. A., & Yell, M. L. (2010). Individualized education programs: Legal requirements and research findings. *Exceptionality*, *18*(3), 109–23. https://doi.org/10.1080/09362835.2010.491740.

Cole, J. S., & Korkmaz, A. (2013). First-year students' psychological well-being and need for cognition: Are they important predictors of academic engagement?

Journal of College Student Development, 54(6), 557–569. https://doi.org/10.1353/csd.2013.0082.

Cronje, J. C. (2017). Learning 3.0: Rhizomatic implications for blended learning. In K. Persichitte, A. Suparman, & M. Spector (Eds.), *Educational technology to improve quality and access on a global scale. Educational communications and technology: Issues and innovations.* Springer. https://doi.org/10.1007/978-3-319-66227-5_2.

Cormier, D. (2008). Rhizomatic education: Community as curriculum. *Innovate 4*(5). http://www.innovateonline.info/index.php?view=article&id=550.

Davidson, D. N., & Gooden, J. S. (2001). Are we preparing beginning principals for the special education challenges they will encounter? *ERS Spectrum, 19*(4), 42–49. https://eric.ed.gov/?id=EJ639030.

Deleuze, G., & Guattari, F. (1988). *A thousand plateaus: Capitalism and schizophrenia.* Bloomsbury Publishing.

Demko, M. (2010). Teachers become zombies: The ugly side of scripted reading curriculum. *Voices from the Middle, 17*(3), 62–64. https://search.proquest.com/docview/213930048?accountid=14745.

Edyburn, D. L. (2010). Would you recognize universal design for learning if you saw it? Ten propositions for new directions for the second decade of UDL. *Learning Disability Quarterly, 33*(1), 33–41. https://doi.org/10.1177/073194871003300103.

Edyburn, D., & Gardner, J. E. (2009). Readings in special education technology: Universal design for learning. *Council for Exceptional Children.*

Friend, M. (2016). Co-teaching as a special education service: Is classroom collaboration a sustainable practice? *Educational Practice and Reform, 2,* 1–12. http://journals.radford.edu/index.php/EPR/article/view/55/29.

Getting Smart, eduInnovation, & Teton Science Schools. (2017, February 9). What is place-based education and why does it matter? https://www.gettingsmart.com/wp-content/uploads/2017/02/What-is-Place-Based-Education-and-Why-Does-it-Matter-3.pdf.

Goodley, D. (2007). Towards socially just pedagogies: Deleuzoguattarian critical disability studies. *International Journal of Inclusive Education, 11*(3), 317–34. http://dx.doi.org/10.1080/13603110701238769.

Goodman, J. I., Hazelkorn, M., Bucholz, J. L., Duffy, M. L., & Kitta, Y. (2011). Inclusion and graduation rates: What are the outcomes? *Journal of Disability Policy Studies, 21*(4), 241–52. https://doi.org/10.1177/1044207310394449.

Hall, T. E., Meyer, A., & Rose, D. H. (Eds.). (2012). *Universal design for learning in the classroom: Practical applications.* Guilford Press.

Hamilton, L., Halverson, R., Jackson, S., Mandinach, E., Supovitz, J., & Wayman, J. (2009). Using student achievement data to support instructional decision making (NCEE 2009-4067). National Center for Education Evaluation and Regional Assistance, Institute of Education Sciences, U.S. Department of Education. Retrieved from http://ies.ed.gov/ncee/wwc/publications/practiceguides/.

Harris, D. (2016). Rhizomatic education and Deleuzian theory. *Open Learning, 31*(3), 219–32. http://dx.doi.org/10.1080/02680513.2016.1205973.

Hitchcock, C., Meyer, A., Rose, D., & Jackson, R. (2002). Providing new access to the general curriculum: Universal design for learning. *Teaching Exceptional Children, 35*(2), 8–17. https://doi.org/10.1177/004005990203500201.

Hodgson, N., & Standish, P. (2009). Uses and misuses of poststructuralism in educational research. *International Journal of Research & Method in Education*, *32*(3), 309–26. https://doi.org/10.1080/17437270903259865.

Jensen, E. (2013). How poverty affects classroom engagement. *Faces of Poverty*, ASCD, *70*(8), 24–30. http://www.ascd.org/publications/educational-leadership/may13/vol70/num08/How-Poverty-Affects-Classroom-Engagement.aspx.

La Salle, T. P., Roach, A. T., & McGrath, D. (2013). The relationship of IEP quality to curricular access and academic achievement for students with disabilities. *International Journal of Special Education*, *28*(1), 135–44. http://files.eric.ed.gov/fulltext/EJ1013681.pdf.

Lowery, K. A., Hollingshead, A., Howery, K., & Bishop, J. B. (2017). More than one way: Stories of UDL and inclusive classrooms. *Research and Practice for Persons with Severe Disabilities*, *42*(4), 225–42. https://doi.org/10.1177/1540796917711668.

Martin, J. L. (2017). Special education in online and virtual school programs. *Richards Lindsay & Martin, L.L.P.* https://www.ksde.org/Portals/0/SES/legal/conf17/Martin VirtualPrograms.pdf.

Mazzotti, V. L., Rowe, D. A., Sinclair, J., Poppen, M., Woods, W. E., & Shearer, M. L. (2016). Predictors of post-school success: A systematic review of NLTS2 secondary analyses. *Career Development and Transition for Exceptional Individuals*, *39*(4), 196–215. https://doi.org/10.1177/2165143415588047.

Murray, R., Shea, M., Shea, B., & Harlin, R. (2004). Issues in education: Avoiding the one-size-fits-all curriculum: Textsets, inquiry, and differentiating instruction. *Childhood Education*, *81*(1), 33–35. https://doi.org/10.1080/00094056.2004.10521291.

National Center for Education Statistics. (2020). The condition of education: Students with disabilities. *Author*. https://nces.ed.gov/programs/coe/pdf/Indicator_CGG/coe_cgg_2016_05.pdf.

Office of Special Education and Rehabilitative Services (OSERS). (2020, March 12). Questions and answers on providing services to children with disabilities during the coronavirus disease 2019 outbreak. https://sites.ed.gov/idea/files/qa-covid-19-03-12-2020.pdf.

Pyle, N., & Wexler, J. (2012). Preventing students with disabilities from dropping out. *Intervention in School and Clinic*, *47*(5), 283–89. https://doi.org/10.1177/1053451211430118.

Rabren, K., Dunn, C., & Chambers, D. (2002). Predictors of post-high school employment among young adults with disabilities. *Career Development for Exceptional Individuals*, *25*(1), 25–40. https://doi.org/10.1177/088572880202500103.

Reeves, S., Bishop, J., & Filce, H. G. (2010). Response to intervention (RtI) and tier systems: Questions remain as educators make challenging decisions. *Delta Kappa Gamma Bulletin*, *76*(4), 30.

Smith Canter, L. L., King, L. H., Williams, J. B., Metcalf, D., & Rhys Myrick Potts, K. (2017). Evaluating pedagogy and practice of Universal Design for Learning in public schools. *Exceptionality Education International*, *27*(1), 1–16. https://ir.lib.uwo.ca/eei/vol27/iss1/1.

Stahl, K., Mellard, D. F., & East, T. B. (n.d.). IDEA opportunities and challenges in online settings. *Office of Special Education and Rehabilitative Services Blog. U.S.*

Department of Education. https://sites.ed.gov/osers/2016/08/idea-opportunities-and-challenges-in-online-settings/.

Sulla, N. (2018). *Students taking charge in grades K-5: Inside the learner-active, technology-infused classroom.* Routledge.

Sullivan, A. L., Van Norman, E. R., & Klingbeil, D. A. (2014). Exclusionary discipline of students with disabilities: Student and school characteristics predicting suspension. *Remedial and Special Education, 35*(4), 199–210. https://doi.org/10.1177/0741932513519825.

The Hunt Institute. (2020, April 1). COVID-19 policy considerations: Support for students with disabilities. *The Intersection.* http://www.hunt-institute.org/resources/2020/04/Covid-19-policy-playbook-support-for-students-with-disabilities/.

Tomlinson, C. A. (2002). Different learners different lessons. *Instructor, 112*(2), 21–25.

U.S. Department of Education. (2010, November 18). Fulfilling the promise of IDEA: Remarks on the 35th anniversary of the Individuals with Disabilities Education Act. https://www.ed.gov/news/speeches/fulfilling-promise-idea-remarks-35th-anniversary-individuals-disabilities-education-act.

Chapter 6

Mental Health Implications for Administrators, Faculty, Students, and Families

Susan Kinsella

Mental health issues related to the pandemic are significant and present numerous challenges to those leading during a crisis. Impact on administrators, teachers, school staff members, students, and families include trauma induced by both short-and long-term isolation and quarantine, practical matters of online teaching and accountability, systemic challenges, and operational needs. This chapter will address each of those areas and look at recommendations moving forward.

Being an educational administrator is a challenging position. On a good day it is necessary to balance the needs of students and the demands of parents, along with the workplace concerns of teachers, clinical school personnel, cafeteria workers, librarians, bus drivers, maintenance workers, and office personnel. Competent school leaders must exhibit excellent communication skills in listening, public speaking, and writing, as well as in problem-solving, assessment, budgeting, and planning. Crises occur impacting schools and the stakeholders in school communities.

The impact of the pandemic in 2020 was an example where the work of a school administrator tripled. Leading during a crisis requires another set of skills. It becomes necessary to make assessments of situations and decisions quicker, know how to collaborate with others to negotiate solutions, locate necessary resources for students, faculty, and staff, and advocate for changes not just during the immediate crisis but for the long term.

Over the past several years, our schools have been faced with numerous challenges from school shootings and violence, bullying, and social media exploitation, to healthcare issues with SARS, and now the COVID-19 pandemic. In a short period of time, our schools have had to adapt to the current situation with students working and learning from home in online environments with their parents and siblings nearby. Consider that some of those students may not have affordable, stable housing and may be living temporarily in hotels, shelters, or with family and friends.

Employed parents may have had to work from home with many distractions and with expectations from schools about assisting their children with lessons. Many unemployed parents were worried about finding another job, paying bills, and trying to get their needs met. Families that were unemployed longer feared the loss of a paycheck, a home, or the lack of a subsidized breakfast and lunch the children received at school. Students who didn't have a computer, technology ability, or other resources in their home, such as Internet, fell behind in their school work and feared failing a subject or the semester in school, making repeat of a grade necessary.

Teachers, eager to assist their students, became frustrated at the lack of resources available to them, or lacked the technological skills themselves if they were not trained in online teaching and learning. Mental health issues related to this pandemic were significant and presented numerous challenges.

The impact on administrators, teachers, school staff members, students, and families includes trauma induced by short- and long-term isolation and quarantine, practical matters of online teaching and accountability, systemic challenges, and operational needs. We will address each one of these issues and then discuss the resources necessary to handle them.

TRAUMA DUE TO ISOLATION AND QUARANTINE

It is often difficult to determine if someone has a mental illness or if their behaviors might be appropriate reactions to a current life situation. Sometimes the result of a physical illness might yield uncharacteristic behaviors like anger, aggression, or hyperactivity. Dealing with those experiencing symptoms of mental illness is difficult, but manageable with specific training in handling the behaviors. According to the National Alliance of Mental Illness (www.nami.org, 2020), common symptoms of mental illness in adolescents and adults can include:

- Anxiety or excessive fears
- Lack of energy, lethargy
- Anger and irritability
- Difficulty sleeping
- Visual or auditory hallucinations
- Inability to function on a daily basis or to handle stress or problems
- Confusion or trouble concentrating
- Substance abuse
- Suicidal thoughts

- Mood changes or feelings of extreme sadness
- Avoidance of friends and social events
- Change in eating habits either eating too much or too little; concern with weight gain
- Change in sex drive

Young children can begin to exhibit mental health issues which usually manifests itself as behavioral symptoms. It is important for young children to learn how to talk about their thoughts and emotions. According to NAMI (2020), some mental health issues seen in children include:

- Changes in school performance
- Inability to control one's behavior, temper tantrums
- Excessive worry or anxiety
- Hyperactive behavior
- Sleep disorders or nightmares
- Frequent disobedience or aggression toward others

Understanding that a student is dealing with a mental illness allows a teacher or administrator to anticipate certain behaviors. However, trauma-induced behaviors due to isolation may be unexpected. Children, adolescents, and adults who shelter in place without interpersonal interactions with others may experience sensory deprivation due to a lack of touching, face-to-face interactions, speaking with others, having others listen to them, or a general lack of the use of the senses—visual, auditory, olfactory, taste, and touch (Lee, 2020).

The recent suicide of a twelve-year-old Ohio boy was determined to be related to the COVID-19 isolation. His father thought he was just withdrawing due to boredom, spending more time in his room alone. In fact, his isolation may have culminated in his trauma-induced suicide (Somerville, 2020).

People with underlying psychological disorders may experience increased levels of fear and anxiety, which can produce strong emotional reactions in children and adults. Outbursts of anger, crying, or argumentative behavior may be experienced. Higher levels of fear, anxiety, and depression can be realized, making it difficult for family members to deal with this additional stress while living in quarantine (Kaushik & Chauhan, 2020).

Relationships became strained and with few places to retreat for privacy, handling emotional crises can be difficult. Parents and caregivers needed additional assistance. Parents trying to balance their work-at-home life with their family responsibilities were unable or ill-equipped to deal with the challenges of multiple school assignments with one or more children at home.

In the *Adverse Childhood Experience Study* (Smith, 2017), researchers studied 26,000 adults and found that adverse childhood experiences (ACEs) were common, hidden, or often unnoticed. Children can be clever at hiding issues they deem shameful, blame themselves for, or fear there may be consequences for. Psychosocial experiences can vary, such as growing up in an abusive home, which demonstrates physical, emotional, or sexual abuse. Equally traumatic can be growing up in a household with an alcoholic, living with a drug user, lacking a parent or guardian, surviving a violent household, having an imprisoned family member, having a mentally ill, chronically depressed, or institutionalized family member, having a mother being treated violently, and/or having both biological parents not present. Any or all of these experiences can be correlated with organic disease, social malfunctions, and mental illness.

These ACEs produce neurodevelopmental and emotional damage and can impair social and school performance. Also, children who are isolated for short or long periods of time, without appropriate social interaction, can experience anxiety, depression, and loss of control. It was found that ACEs can have a profound effect up to fifty years later. At this point, these psychosocial experiences can manifest themselves into organic disease, social malfunction, and mental illness and can shape adult life.

ACEs are the main determinant of the health and social well-being of the nation. Primary prevention is possible and the literature suggests doing numerous screenings for ACEs with children through common medical evaluations. As a nation, we need to be aware of this mental health issue and approach the solution with multiple resources. First we need to identify high-risk students, use a valid assessment tool, develop a treatment plan for the student and their family, and provide referrals to community agencies and local mental health services. Schools can also add more mental health services and develop peer-support services in the schools, such as bullying prevention programs (Ko et al., 2008).

During the pandemic we needed to consider that children or teens may have been sequestered in a violent household with dysfunctional family members who suffer from mental illness or alcoholism (Fegert et al., 2020). We saw the additional stressors of national protests due to the death of George Floyd, a forty-six-year-old black man, who was arrested by police and then held down against his will despite pleas for help. Videos of this scene have played out across America in televisions, online, and in other media forms.

Children, adolescents, and adults were susceptible to these images and what they mean. What families or other household members are sharing about this event, their views on race, gender, or political viewpoints, and solutions to issues of social injustice or perceived injustices are concerning.

Children or adults may be housed with people they admire but who have no tolerance for different racial, gender, religious, or political viewpoints. In fact, their solutions may be prejudicial or discriminatory and involve violence or other forms of social injustice. Children returning to school from these environments may have difficulty aligning their newfound beliefs with those of their classmates or school officials who are creating new curricula on social acceptance, open dialogue, and classroom discussion of these issues.

For instance, in 2015, twenty-one-year-old Dylann Roof was arrested for the murder of nine African Americans in South Carolina in one of the largest mass murders in American history inside a house of worship. Dylann was a self-proclaimed white supremacist, with a hate agenda and a website manifesto published before the shooting. Along with his written hate journals, he espoused belief in the Confederate flag and the supremacy of the white race. Many have asked where he learned those ideals and how he became susceptible at such a young age. There has been growing concern over these solid convictions of far-right terrorists in the United States and the etiology of those beliefs.

These are the kinds of issues that school districts will be dealing with as children return to school after the pandemic and in the future. With school violence an issue in the not too distant past, we were confronted daily with how to keep students safe in the classroom and not become victims of violence, prejudice, bullying, and other discriminatory practices.

The conversation needs to get stepped up a notch after the isolation of COVID. We need to focus on identifying administrative strategies to improve overall safety in our schools.

STRATEGIES

Healthy child development includes social interaction and play, which impacts a child's cognitive, linguistic, and social-emotional development. The concern is that many children during this pandemic are now socially isolated and cut off from school, friends, and other positive social contacts. Parents and teachers need to be aware of the impact of social isolation on children and keep them connected to their friends and classmates, so they can see others are ok. Use of Zoom, FaceTime, and other forms of social media is important for all age groups but especially for children whose development is based upon this interaction (Stecklein, 2020).

In an article by Gulino (2020), Joseph McGuire, a child psychologist with Johns Hopkins University, suggests that people working with children pay particular attention to their concerns over the coronavirus. Children viewing numerous news programs about the rising death toll and hearing family members' concerns over the pandemic may become extremely anxious over losing their loved ones and, in general, feel a lack of control over the situation. It is important to listen to your child's concern, correcting any misinformation and helping to eliminate immediate fears. It is equally important to talk with them and not be dismissive of their concerns.

Many adults feel the same way. Information from reliable sources should be shared and discussed as a family, highlighting the positive aspects of the illness like sharing more quality family time. Too much time in front of television or computer screens can increase anxiety, as numerous programs on the coronavirus and its negative impact could cause problems. Obsession with the news media or sensational highlights of the illness should be avoided, so monitoring the screen time for all family members is recommended.

Instead, focus on the fact that family members can share some valuable time together. It was a time when children gain some control over their situation by learning how to protect themselves. Teaching them how to wash their hands throughout the day, making sure they spend the accurate amount of time and attention to doing so, can help curtail the illness. Focus on prevention and the idea of safe distancing, wearing of masks when it is necessary to be away from the home, and taking care of yourself physically and mentally are all good safeguards against contracting the disease.

All of these measures will heighten a child's sense of control and help to decrease the feelings of anxiety and panic. Being knowledgeable and prepared are important ingredients to ward off panic. Understand that anxiety and panic are really signs of the loss of control that need to be reestablished (www.ox.ac.uk/news/2020-03-31).

A useful tool for parents, caregivers, and teachers to use is the concept of mindfulness. This technique can help children and adults reduce stress by focusing on the present situation and stopping to sit quietly and to focus on their breathing, taking deep breaths in and slowly expelling their breaths as they concentrate on their surroundings, count to ten, or just relax. This simple method of relaxation will slow the heart rate and allow them to gain control over their emotions and the rising anxiety and panic that may be setting in.

This is an important tool for anyone dealing with family, friends, or loved ones who experience debilitating episodes of anxiety or panic attacks. As a social worker, in my work with children and adults, and later as a parent, I often found it helpful to "reset." A simple "Can we start over and do this a different way, please?" would often get my clients or children to understand they had the power to control their behavior and we could start over, so they could "do it better." This technique worked so much better than reprimanding, arguing, and then often escalating a situation that could have been modified with a simple do-over. Just relax, take deep breaths, and think about how to start over in a more controlled manner without letting our sometimes irrational thoughts and destructive behaviors carry us away.

Remember that stress impacts the immune system. Any upheavals to the immune system now are not needed. Keeping your immune system in tip top shape with healthy habits, a positive attitude, and reduced levels of stress will help in increasing your protection from the illness. Studying earlier periods of quarantine gives us information on what to expect as we move forward after this pandemic.

After the SARS epidemic, it was reported that those who were quarantined were two to three times more likely to have symptoms of posttraumatic stress disorder (PTSD). In studies in both China and Canada, those people who had been isolated still practiced distancing of others and were slow to return to normal daily living. Children in quarantine were four times more likely to suffer PTSD. Over 28 percent of those quarantined were later diagnosed with a trauma-related mental health disorder (Douglas, 2020). According to the World Health Organization, quarantine and social isolation time should be filled with new and positive experiences that engage individuals in physical, cognitive, relaxation exercises, reading, and entertainment (www.who.int, 2020).

ONLINE TEACHING AND ACCOUNTABILITY

Workers experiencing mental health issues due to COVID-19 need assistance as well (Greenwood, 2020). Administrators dealing with student and family issues also have to consider the additional burden teachers felt as they adjust to teaching online and working in a new environment. This means that students often had their parents or siblings present during a lesson, making paying attention difficult.

In many schools, teachers were not knowledgeable about how to teach effectively online, or to children with little or no resources at home. Some schools provided computers for their stay at home students, but many schools throughout the country could not afford to provide computers for their students. Many teachers provided their students with the resources they needed, often paying for items themselves.

Teachers across the country attended to families in car lines coming to school for USDA lunches or additional food bags that the community provided. School administrators had worked to ensure that their students had the necessary provisions for learning while at school or at home. This additional burden of assisting families who were often left unemployed, isolated, and with several children to care for was stressful.

As each state mandated stay at home orders with the intended outcome of a slower spread of the contagious disease, mental health professionals reported these measures can have psychological impacts. Social distancing and quarantine measures created feelings of depression and isolation, warns Dr. Tandon, head of psychiatry at Western Michigan University School of Medicine (Krafcik, 2020).

Anxiety develops with a disruption in a regular schedule creating a sense of loss of control and depression. Although everyone is at risk, some people are particularly vulnerable, such as older people and those with compromised immune systems, children who worry the isolation will never end and miss playing with friends, teens who feel the loss of significant events like proms and graduation, and those with underlying mental health issues or substance abuse (Liacko, 2020).

There was also concern for the frontline workers who worked diligently to serve others like doctors, healthcare workers, first responders, and our teachers. As children were moved online to finish the school year, teachers across the country had to adapt quickly to changing routines, move curriculum for on-ground classes to an online format, and then begin to teach to children at home through a virtual medium such as Zoom, Microsoft Teams, or something similar.

Often parents were called upon to assist, so teachers were now handling children and parents on the home computer. There was significant stress as states decided if children would return to the classroom to finish the year or finish online. Teachers had to work hard to ensure their students were learning the material and were capable of passing tests and moving forward. This additional pressure upon classroom teachers can create an overwhelming sense of failure if classroom expectations are not achieved, adding additional anxiety and stress to an already difficult situation.

As leaders, school administrators must support their worker's mental health, especially during a crisis. This could be accomplished by first promoting employee assistance programs (EAPs) in their district. These programs can connect school district employees to counselors who can assist them with issues related to mental health, childcare, marriage and family counseling, elder care, food resources, and even medical bills and insurance issues. It has been noted that although many organizations have EAPs in place, the average utilization rate is only about 4.5 percent (Wingard, 2020).

Mind Share Partners, a training and advising organization to support workplace mental health, completed a study in 2019 on its member organizations (Greenwood et al., 2019). Results indicated 80 percent of workers still see a stigma associated with seeking out mental health services at work. This perception of shame prevents them from reaching out for professional help in the workplace. Also significant was the fact that workers were two times as likely to assist a coworker with an issue than to share their own mental health concern or seek treatment themselves. Only 37 percent of workers saw their organizational leaders as supporters for mental health services at work.

The United States is clearly behind our Canadian, Australian, and United Kingdom colleagues, who lead the way in workplace mental health services. American workers clearly stated they wanted more mental health training, more information on resources, and a workplace environment that was supportive of their needs in mental health (www.nsc.org, 2020).

SYSTEMATIC CHALLENGES

Mental health practitioners who understand trauma have called for a System Change, which requires a comprehensive look at *students, the school environment, resources, and community partnerships*. This had happened when other crises, like school violence, have impacted schools. It is apparent there will be a need for more mental health services for our students after this pandemic, and we need to consider what approaches administrators can take to be prepared for a System Change.

The idea of developing an interdisciplinary approach that includes administration, faculty, parents, students, and community partners should be considered. This collaborative approach requires educators, administrators, social workers, health and mental health professionals, and religious leaders to partner. The idea of a school-community partnership with service, civic, religious, and others is necessary for the coordination of resources for high-risk students and for access to referral of community mental health services for students, teachers, district employees, and administrators (Wood and Kinsella, 2018).

Anticipating the additional need for mental health services after the pandemic included continued funding for these resources and ongoing evaluation of these services. An interdisciplinary school crisis team could be utilized to review the crisis response plan and then decide how to move forward. A school crisis could be defined in a variety of ways, such as violence in our schools, PTSD, habitual bullying, chronic health issues of students, failing scores on standardized tests, and unusual episodes of issues like the coronavirus, which sent students home to finish classroom learning online.

How prepared are districts to handle any of these situations? We were all amazed with the speed and resiliency of our teachers and administrators as they moved their classrooms online and continued full day Zoom or Microsoft Teams classes for months. For some this model worked well, but other students fell through the cracks without the direct assistance of the teacher, or an updated computer, or the Internet.

School districts need to consider their policies and procedures and work collaboratively with their communities to develop a framework for administrative change. Partnerships among schools, community agencies, students, and parents are necessary for significant change (Aefsky et al., 2017). Regional districts should work together to secure funding for additional services like medical or mental health and emergency services. Advocacy for new state and federal policies can be garnered with the assistance of school and community coalitions. Best practices should address the use of school assessments and referral services. With the knowledge that ACEs create trauma leading to neurodevelopmental and emotional damage, high-risk students should be identified, assessed, and treated.

Primary prevention should include the identification of all high-risk students who may have underlying trauma due to an adverse childhood experience or residual effects of the pandemic, before any maladaptive behavior begins. Classroom discussions on issues of social justice and new ideas for curriculum changes like "reformative justice" or "restorative justice" could be considered. More school districts are implementing restorative justice practices (RJPs) and bullying prevention (BP) strategies that encourage productive student behavior. RJPs are responsive strategies to address conflict, build relationships, and create a sense of community (Swain-Bradway & Sisaye, 2016).

What kinds of services could we support in a Systems Change Effort? Several employers are supporting more vigorous mental health programs for employees during this pandemic. At Mental Health America, several businesses and organizations have been reported in their blog regarding innovative EAP practices (Adams, 2020). These include such initiatives as:

- Live meditation sessions and activity breaks
- Resiliency and stress management activities
- Morale-boosting activities
- Newsletters
- Podcasts
- Zoom book clubs
- Meditation sessions
- Animal therapy
- Manager well-being calls
- Weekly self-care videos
- 1:1 health coaching for employees and their spouses
- Weekly well-being communications

These innovative types of services can be adapted for people of all ages and can be useful in our schools. They are also cost-effective and easy to deliver in the classroom, the individual school, or throughout a district.

OPERATIONAL NEEDS

As we consider the human element impacted by the pandemic, we have to look at vulnerable populations like the elderly people in senior living arrangements that were recognized early one in the illness. Depicted as the most vulnerable, we soon learned that certain ethnic groups, those with compromised immune systems, and people young and old were also victims. Finding appropriate information on how to protect ourselves and who to believe in the political arena or on the news broadcast was confusing. The scope of the virus was unsettling as it traveled around the globe and one by one countries shut down.

After weeks in insolation, it is now apparent that we needed to be better prepared for another round of this illness or one like it. As a country, we needed to have a better safety net and a collaboration of economic, political, religious, educational, and emergency organizations that are focused on working together and making sure that as citizens we are protected. That means that we needed to have policies in place to move quickly and transparently from work to home, with equal resources for everyone, including food, housing, medical access, and enough supplies, with safe and better outcomes.

As a school district, that meant that we must work together within our counties and states to ensure that all children receive equal access to resources and stable online learning. Teachers need to be prepared to teach online when necessary and must be trained in advance of program delivery. Human resource departments, finance offices, curriculum and instruction departments, and safety teams have to collaborate to develop plans, so we are prepared to move forward. Having the knowledge from this quarantine, we can better prepare for the next emergency knowing that it can be done efficiently and effectively.

RECOMMENDATIONS FOR PHYSICAL AND MENTAL HEALTH

According to a report published by the Partnership Center, a branch of the U.S. Department of Health and Human Services, a recent survey by the American Psychiatric Association found that almost half of all Americans were extremely anxious about contracting the coronavirus and about 40 percent are worried about dying from the illness. A bigger concern was the anxiety over family members getting the coronavirus (www.hhs.gov, 2020). How are people coping now? It was found that 25 percent of people turned to their faith and leaders in their church before looking to mental health practitioners (www.hhs.gov, 2020).

Keeping people involved with their church, synagogue, or temple is extremely important during this time of isolation. Many services are taking place online through Zoom gatherings. Whatever medium can be used to connect people with those leaders whom they trust is essential at this time. Allowing children, adolescents, adults, or the elderly to engage in online or telephone discussions with religious leaders they trust can assist in alleviating loneliness, anxiety, and depression.

Many resources were developed quickly for people to get a better understanding of the COVID virus, how it could impact you and your family, and ways to remain safe. An uptick was also noticed in the number of telehealth services for mental health (Porterfield, 2020). As the number of infected people began to rise, it was obvious this was an illness that was not restricted to one community or region of the country. The number of fatalities increased causing people across the nation to consider the best course of action for them and their families.

One by one states began to close and order shelter in place restrictions, as a precaution against the further spread of the disease. Daily news programs accounted for the increasing number of those impacted nationally, along with the mounting increase in those losing jobs with dire economic results. Although the media often used the tag "we're all in this together," it may not have seemed that way to single people isolated in apartments in urban settings or for rural families with few resources near them.

Many organizations did rise to the occasion with numerous websites provided for people of all ages with activities, concerts, free museum tours, and free movies or streaming. New traditions were quickly established to honor healthcare workers in cities large and small by gathering at 7 p.m. each evening on balconies, open windows, or doors, and engaging in making noise, singing songs, or waving flags. All of this demonstrated the human need to stay connected. This came at a time when people were being quarantined due to their positive result on a COVID test, or self-isolated, as required by local and state authorities in an effort to keep the disease from spreading.

News stories harkened back to 1918 and the time of the Spanish Flu, giving us hope that we could get through this as our ancestors had before us. What lessons had we learned? The World Health Organization developed a website chock full of recommendations for *physical health, mental health, parenting, healthy eating,* and *smoking cessation* as means of coping with the COVID virus as people isolated (www.who.int).

Other organizations followed suit giving an array of online activities, Zoom meetings, story hours, cooking lessons, and bird watching, to name just a few. Some people responded by trying new things with surprising results. New talents were discovered like gardening, drawing, and baking, while traditional family activities like board games, puzzles, and cards became popular again.

PHYSICAL HEALTH

Staying in shape physically is always recommended, but this is especially important during the pandemic. Just a few minutes a day of stretching, walking, or aerobic activity can clear your mind, help you to focus on yourself, and give you more energy. People who exercise improve their blood circulation and muscle activity. A regular routine of some physical activity can reduce blood pressure and the risks associated with stroke and heart attack, as well as maintaining a proper weight. Staying physically fit has been shown to prevent type 2 diabetes and some cancers and can also prevent vulnerability to COVID-19 (www.who.int, 2020).

Physical activity has also been shown to improve a sense of well-being. People sleep better at night, have better memories, are more relaxed, and overall feel better about themselves reducing depression and anxiety. Exercise helps your body to release endorphins in the brain, which help you to relax and impact your nervous system and other internal organs in a positive way, reducing stress. Having a daily routine of some kind of physical activity will give those quarantined a sense of purpose and help us to have positive interpersonal activities with those in the quarantined space. Indoor exercises or a daily walk outdoors can do wonders for our disposition and give us a new focus.

Regardless of their age, people need to have some kind of regular daily exercise for themselves and for those in isolation with them. Consider those in your home—infants should be active several times a day and at least thirty minutes as floor time, children under five should have three hours a day of various types of play, children and adolescents five to seventeen years of age should spend at least one hour a day in vigorous activity, and those over age eighteen should have 2.5 hours per week of physical activity.

MENTAL HEALTH

According to the World Health Organization (www.who.int, 2020), the speed with which we moved to safe shelter to prevent the coronavirus from spreading, along with the lack of physical contact with our family, friends, and colleagues, will take time to get used to. This rapid change to a different lifestyle, while also managing the fear and anxiety of worrying about ourselves or family members contracting the illness, makes us feel vulnerable and very stressed. Those with existing mental health conditions can find this extremely difficult (www.ama-assn.org, 2020).

Some suggestions to help normalize the situation for everyone included having a routine, keep a regular bedtime, maintain personal hygiene, eat healthy meals, exercise, set aside time to work and time to rest, do things you enjoy for part of the day, be aware of how much you watch, and listen or attend to the news. Be sure to stay connected to family and friends by phone, email, or other forms of social media.

Limit your alcohol intake or don't drink at all out of boredom, fear, or anxiety. Take regular screen breaks from computers, and don't spend too much time on video games. Keep your social media contacts positive, and if possible support others in your community. Make sure you have family discussions about the coronavirus and ask how individual members are feeling, so you can discuss those emotions. Do creative things each day that appeals to you and your family like games, outdoor activities, drawing, use of music, gardening, or baking.

Support at home: Plan time to have fun with your family. Make sure family members who need medication continue to take it as needed. Those in substance abuse programs may find it harder to stay compliant while they have increased feelings of anxiety, fear, and isolation. Call your healthcare provider if stress prevents you from functioning normally (www.who.int, 2020).

Everyone feels differently after coming out of quarantine. The CDC recommendations (www.cdc.gov, 2020) indicate that some of those feelings may be a relief at the end of quarantine but still a worry of your own health or those of others, stress over self-monitoring, anger at others' unfounded fears of contracting the disease from you, guilt over not be able to work, frustration over dealing with children and family issues, and other emotional changes.

The CDC offered links to resources for children, teens, adults, and families on their website (www.cdc.gov, 2020). It is always best to seek out and use the available resources for ourselves or for others who are in need.

REFERENCES

Adams, T. (2020).Workplace wellness. *Mental Health America*. https://www.mhanational.org/taylor-adams.

Aefsky, F., Lamb, J., Laroche, D., Sedlack, R., & Zetsche, T. (2017). K-12 school partnerships. In Aefsky, F. (Ed.), *Collaborative leadership: Building capacity through effective partnerships* (pp. 33–52). Rowman & Littlefield.

CDC (Centers for Disease Control and Prevention). (n.d.). Adverse childhood experiences (ACEs). https://www.cdc.gov/violenceprevention/acestudy/.

Considering faith, community, and mental health during COVID-19 crisis, The Partnership Center, U.S. Department of Health and Human Services. (April 2, 2020). https://www.hhs.gov/sites/default/files/4-2-2020-mental-health-covid-final.pdf.

Coronavirus Disease 2019 (COVID-19) Coping with Stress. Centers for Disease Control and Prevention. (2020). https://www.cdc.gov/coronavirus/2019-ncov/daily-life-coping/managing-stress-anxiety.html.

Coronavirus Disease 2019 (COVID-19) Resources. Centers for Disease Control and Prevention. (2020). https://www.cdc.gov/coronavirus/2019-ncov/php/contact-tracing/contact-tracingplan/resources.html.

Douglas, Yellowlees. (April 2020). The costs of social isolation: Loneliness and COVID-19. *Psychiatry Advisor, Haymarket Media*. https:/www.psychiatryadviser.com/home/topics/general-psychiatry/costs-of-social-isolation-lonliness-covid19/.

Fegert, J. M., Vitiello, B., Plener, P. L., & Clemens, V. (2020). Challenges and burden of the coronavirus 2019 (COVID-19) pandemic for child and adolescent mental health: A narrative review to highlight clinical and research needs in the acute phase and the long return to normality. *Child and Adolescent Psychiatry and Mental Health 14*, 20. https://doi.org/10.1186/s13034-020-00329-3.

Greenwood, K. (2020). How to lead with mental health in mind during the coronavirus pandemic. *Forbes. Mind Share Partners.* March 19. forbes.com/sites/mindsharepartners/2020/03/19/how-to-lead-with-mental-health-in-mind-during-the-coronavirus-pandemic/#23460e702f35.

Greenwood, K., Bapat, V., & Maughan, M. (2019). Research: People want their employers to talk about mental health. *Harvard Business Review*, November 11. https://hbr.org/2019/10/research-people-want-their-employers-to-talk-about-mental-health.

Gulino, E. (2020). How to help someone with anxiety, according to mental health experts. *Refinery 29,* May 5.

Healthy at home—physical activity. World Health Organization. (2020). https://www.who.int/news-room/campaigns/connecting-the-world-to-combat-coronavirus/healthyathome---physical-activity.

Importance of effective communication with children about COVID-19 to protect mental health, University of Oxford, News and Event, March 31, 2020. http://www.ox.ac.uk/news/2020-03-31-importance-effective-communication-children-about-covid-19-protect-mental-health.

Kaushik, Chatterjee, & Chauhan, V. S. (2020). Epidemics, quarantine, and mental health. *Medical Journal Armed Forces India, 76*(2), 125–27. Published online April 22. https://www.ncbi.nlm.nih.gov/pmc/articles/PMC7176378/.

Ko, S. J., Ford, J. D., Kassam-Adams, N., Berkowitz, S. J., Wilson, C., Wong, M., & Layne, C. M. (2008). Creating trauma-informed systems: Child welfare, education, first responders, health care, and juvenile justice. *Professional Psychology: Research and Practice, 39*(4), 396–404. http://dx.doi.org/10.1037/0735-7028.39.4.396.

Krafcik, M. (2020). State of mind: COVID-19 related disruptions impact mental health. *News Channel 3.* March 30. https://wwmt.com/news/state-of-mind/state-of-mind-03-30-2020.

Lee, J. (2020). COVID 19's mental health effects by age group: children, college age students, working age adults, and older adults. *Healio Psychiatry.* April. https://www.healio.com/news/psychiatry/20200408/covid19s-mental-health-effects-by-age-group-children-college-students-workingage-adults-and-older-ad.

Liacko, A. (2020). How self-quarantine impacts teens and adults' mental health differently, *Fox 5, Atlanta News*. March. https://www.fox5atlanta.com/news/how-self-quarantine-impacts-teens-and-adults-mental-health-differently.

Managing mental health during Covid-19. *AMA Public Health.* June 5, 2020. https://www.ama-assn.org/delivering-care/public-health/managing-mental-healthdu covid19.

Porterfield, C. (2020). Coronavirus: 36% of Americans say pandemic has made a serious impact on their mental health. https://www.forbes.com/sites/carlieporterfield/2020/04/02/coronavirus-36-of-americans-say-pandemic-has-made-a-serious-impact-on-their-mental-health/#6738e60d6c8e.

Resources for employee mental health and well being. National Safety Council. (2020). https://www.nsc.org/work-safety/safety-topics/coronavirus/mental-health-and-wellbeing.

Smith, L. (2017). Combating toxic stress in St. Petersburg. Johns Hopkins All Children's Hospital leads effort to raise awareness about adverse childhood experiences and their damaging impact. *Johns Hopkins Medicine. Community Issue*. https://www.hopkinsmedicine.org/news/articles/combating-toxic-stress-in-st-petersburg.

Somerville, B. (2020). Ohio State alum share story of child's suicide. *WBNS*, Ohio, May. https://www.10tv.com/article/ohio-state-alum-shares-story-childs-suicide-tells-parents-covid-19-isolation-real-2020-may.

Stecklein, Janelle. (2020). COVID-19 is expected to have a long-term mental health impact. *Enid News & Eagle*, Enid, Oklahoma. April. https://www.enidnews.com/virus/covid-19-is-expected-to-have-long-term-mental-health-impact/article_9b67b080-5ac3-52a3 936c43938c648747.html.

Swain-Bradway, J., & Sisaye, S. (2016). Restorative justice practices and bullying prevention. https://www.stopbullying.gov/blog/2016/03/02/restorative-justice-practices-and- bullying-prevention.html.

Warning signs and symptoms. National Alliance on Mental Illness. (2020). https://www.nami.org/About-Mental-Illness/Warning-Signs-and-Symptoms.

Wingard, J. (2020). Leading in the Covid-19 context. *Forbes*. March. https://www.forbes.com/sites/jasonwingard/2020/03/20/mental-health-in-the-workplace-leading-in-times-of-crisis/#5ad7582e6a1b.

Wood, N., & Kinsella, S. (2018). Addressing school violence through interdisciplinary systems change. In Aefsky, F. (Ed.), *Can we ensure safe schools? A collaborative guide on focused strategies for school safety*. Rowman & Littlefield.

Chapter 7

Crisis Management: Operational Challenges for Educational Leaders

Jodi Lamb, Ed Dadez, & Fern Aefsky

This chapter provides a framework for leaders to use when managing any crisis. Each time a crisis occurs, educational leaders face challenges. At times, the challenges are relatively localized, such as a school shooting. Other times, the crisis may have more of a regional impact, such as during California wildfires or hurricanes that make landfall. In fewer situations, a crisis has a national or global impact such as with H1N1 or the COVID-19 pandemic. Regardless of the immediate impact, state and local officials are expected to implement new safety measures that are a direct result of the crisis that occurred and policy and legislative changes that ensued.

A closer look at school shootings provides insight on how a localized event impacted state and national changes. After the Sandy Hook shooting in 2012, policies regarding new school construction morphed into ones that were much more focused on the hardening of the building and providing limited access. These changes transcended state and county lines and are evident on a national scale. After the Parkland shooting in Florida in 2018 and the political visibility of the survivors, state guidelines changed the expectation for law enforcement on campus and generated a strong awareness of mental health issues in schools.

On a regional perspective, schools often bear a burden of providing normalcy to students. After natural disasters such as Hurricanes Katrina and Maria, school districts across the country had to quickly adjust to a growing number of new students as the families evacuated from Louisiana and Puerto Rico. Since the infrastructure in both cases was destroyed, teams were assembled nationally to help get these communities back on their feet (Sarker & Lester, 2019). But in both cases, many families chose to leave as it was not safe, especially for children. These families had lost everything, so the burden to the social systems other than education was also taxed. Mental health issues and providing appropriate care became a focus as students and their families dealt with grief and loss (Jaycox et al., 2007).

As leaders facilitate crisis management teams, a good framework to use is a SWOT analysis. SWOT analyses identify the organization's strengths, weaknesses, opportunities, and threats (SWOT) for stakeholders. As reported by Schooley (2019), this framework enables leaders to identify needs of an organization in order to help develop a plan of action. While this has been a framework used for developing goals and long-term planning, it is a good technique to implement during crisis management and control.

Strategic planning and management involves leaders creating a mechanism to analyze circumstances, create implementation plans for change, make decisions that will be evaluated in a cyclic manner, and facilitate organization leaders' ability to make sound decisions for stakeholders (Gurel & Tat, 2017). This chapter identifies practitioners' questions and concerns in dealing with the physical school building, resource allocation, and components of human resources, in order to deal with any crisis that may occur.

The global pandemic of 2019–2020 created an emergent need for strong leadership and crisis management. As discussed in previous chapters, educational leaders had to manage this crisis for students, staff, families, and faculty as an immediate health crisis dictated.

On a national and global perspective, the world dealt with a wide variety of effects of the COVID-19 pandemic. A struggling economy, high unemployment rates, strained social systems, mental health concerns due to isolation, and a stigmatization (McCauley et al. 2013) toward Asian individuals are elements school officials must be prepared to address. These elements are not new. A look back at how this country addressed the H1N1 pandemic in 2009 showed startling similarities. Even a look at lessons learned from the recent, great recession can give us insights on the slow rebound that should be expected as we recover globally from the COVID-19 pandemic, especially for minorities (Cohen & Casselman, 2020).

As the country slowly emerged from the first phase of the COVID-19 pandemic and looked forward to operating in a new normal, the leadership in many school districts and universities braced for the need to make tough and challenging decisions that range from the way instruction should be provided to how they will balance their budgets. This chapter will explore the impact decisions made at the district, state, and federal level had on schools and universities.

Many questions had to be addressed by educational leaders. Each question posed had different answers as changes occurred. At the point of this chapter being prepared for publication, many states had provided school districts with guidance on procedures for reopening of schools, some schools had reopened, resulting in other challenges that leaders had to content with locally. There were lawsuits, some for and some against schools reopening. There were medical issues of faculty, staff, and children. Many medical experts disagreed on protocols, and where there was agreement, some of those protocols were not followed due to politically motivated challenges.

Changes to guiding documents were ongoing and changed rapidly based on medical, political, and social variables. While many educational leaders tried to keep political and bureaucratic issues separate from their work at hand, it was impossible to do so when those leaders had to follow various mandates given. This impacted colleges and universities and PK-12 school systems nationwide.

COLLEGES AND UNIVERSITIES—ED DADEZ

Over 4,000 college and university leadership teams and task forces were extremely busy, developing and redeveloping plans to address closing, opening, and/or reopening of their organizations. Business affairs, academic affairs, student affairs, athletics, university advancement, and enrollment management were diligently establishing divisional plans, which were then approved by the president and leadership teams, to implement and manage in their respective areas. There were new procedures, processes, and policies put in place to ensure the health, safety, and wellness of students, faculty, staff, and administrators.

Bacevice (2020) contacted students and "asked them what they want their schools to do to ensure the health and wellbeing of everyone on campus. Overall students would like clear direction from their schools, a plan to keep the community safe, and they suggest that those plans adhere to—if not supersede—CDC [Centers for Disease Control and Prevention] or local guidelines." Students believed that the following four recommendations must be sufficiently addressed to ensure everyone at the college and university's health and wellness is taken into full and complete consideration. They were cleaning and sanitizing; COVID-19 testing and doing temperature checks; distance and online learning; and wearing masks and gloves.

These recommendations along with how colleges and universities dealt with financial concerns; faculty and classrooms; student room and board revenue losses; athletics; and possible COVID-19 outbreaks were priorities that every president and leadership team grappled with for the 2020–2021 school year. College and university presidents and their leadership teams were in a precarious situation. They found ways to balance university financial risks with health-related risks of students, faculty, staff, and administrators when both were critically important for the institution. Every college and university had to develop plans to determine if their institution would be able to manage, survive, and thrive in the future.

Lederman (2020) reported that "[p]residents seem relatively sure that they will face financial difficulties. Asked to rate their level of concern about a list of potential issues, 91 percent of presidents said they were very (50 percent) or somewhat concerned about declines in future student enrollment, and 88 percent expressed concern about overall financial stability (31 percent said they were very concerned). Eighty-one percent expressed concern about their ability to afford to employ faculty and staff members."

These financial concerns dictated a careful review of budget items and every line item needed to be placed under review to determine if it should be kept or cut out of the budget. Short-term and long-term capital projects; ongoing campus or off-campus operations; divisional operating budgets; overall staffing; adjunct faculty; academic majors that have low enrollments; and smaller but expensive athletic teams were all at risk.

It was believed that enrollments would be down, which caused budget shortfalls, since having less students means there was less revenue. Room and board was a critical line item in university budgets. With less students on campus, it was difficult to offset this loss of revenue.

The increased or additional costs for ongoing COVID-19 testing were extensive, including temperature checks taken when individuals go into campus buildings; additional cleaning of classrooms, residence halls, and bathrooms by an increased number of housekeeping staff; hand sanitizer stations; and distribution of face masks. Thus there was a need to restructure budgets.

Colleges and universities across the country had to develop options for courses, offering all classes online, face-to-face, or blended. Many institutions considered a mixture of online and in-person classes. Others were experimenting with the idea of having classes with two identified cohorts with one half of the students being in the class and the other half participating virtually. In this model, the two cohorts would change every other day either being in the classroom or virtually.

Some colleges planned to extend the day by offering classes earlier or longer during the week as well as on Saturdays to lessen the number of students heading in and out of classroom buildings. This would reduce class sizes as well as shrink the number of students physically in classes. Another plan being considered to decrease the number of students on campus is to bring freshmen and juniors in the fall and sophomores and seniors in the spring to lessen the campus density.

A number of colleges and universities cancelled their fall study abroad programs based on travel plans, flights, visas, health, and safety, as well as some countries not allowing foreigners to enter their country. There was concern that if there was a second COVID-19 wave, students could be stuck in their study abroad country without a means to return home. Additionally, many international students did not return for the same reason. They either chose to stay in their home countries or were not permitted back to the United States. "The Student and Exchange Visitor Program allowed international student to take more online courses than normal for the spring and summer. But these leadership decisions meant students in fully online programs will need to transfer to a college with in-person courses or leave the U.S., IUCE said" (IHE Staff, July 7, 2020). This was possible for many undergraduates but difficult for graduate and doctoral students who were in the middle of their academic programs or working on their thesis or dissertation with a faculty advisor. "Thus many colleges are likely to be forced this fall into the Sophie's choice of moving online to protect health and chasing away their international students, or keeping those students and making more people sick. Worse, international students might be forced to choose between their health and their education" (Rosenberg, 2020). There were legal challenges to this new guidance by a host of colleges, universities, and professional organizations.

Problems of maintaining social distancing in campus dining halls, snack bars, coffeehouses, and restaurants existed. Colleges and universities personnel decreased the number of tables and chairs to provide appropriate social distancing, but everyone typically wants to eat at the same time. Dining hall staff needed to increase the hours to handle all students and possibly not allow faculty and staff to eat in the dining hall. Paper plates, plastic tableware, and plastic cups were used to ensure one use only.

Athletic programs were significantly impacted. The Ivy League and the Division III Centennial Conference have already cancelled all fall sports. The Big Ten decided not to play any of their out-of-conference football games. A number of other individual colleges have cancelled football games.

The leadership challenge was the negative effect this will have on athletic budgets as well as college and university budgets. For a number of the Power Five schools, football pays for the rest of the athletic department sports as well as a healthy contribution to the university. Not having football in the fall caused a number of institutions to cut athletic programs based on athletic department deficits.

University advancement and enrollment leaders faced challenges as people are hesitant to part with their money with a looming threat of another recession, limited resources due to loss of jobs, and other economic factors. The result was less funds available for student scholarships, at a time when more students needed financial support.

This would assist many students whose parents were furloughed or became unemployed because of COVID-19. Enrollment management will be less stable, as students have many choices for virtual education that did not exist prior to the pandemic. Others decided to go to a community college for a year, gain academic credits, live safely at home, save money, and then head off to other universities.

In addition to having students being safe on campus, colleges and universities needed to ensure that their faculty and staff were safe and protected. To provide social distancing, work from home policies needed to be flexible. For vulnerable faculty, the opportunity to virtually teach was a safer way to provide in-person instruction and teaching.

It was important to have clear, informative communication channels for all campus constituencies. Constant, consistent, and proactive communication is imperative. Leaders needed to be transparent, engage others, and build relationships so that, as in any crisis, management is responsible for ensuring a safe environment for all.

In every emergency situation such as hurricanes, school safety, previous health issues, and racial conflicts, the president and leadership team has to be actively involved in decision making. Additionally, standard operating procedures (SOPs) should be written to handle all types of emergency situations. These SOPs should be reviewed on an ongoing basis, and after action reports should include a discussion of what worked and what needs to be changed for the next emergency.

Policies and procedures should already be in place to manage a myriad of issues that one would need to handle crisis issues. There should be SOPs for hospital contacts, medical testing, hospital transportation, quarantine student and roommates, parental contact, identification of essential staff to be onsite in emergencies, communication channels, and so on.

One of the most important factors in any emergency situation is that students, staff, and faculty trust those making the decisions. As it has been said many times before, trust is not given, it is earned. Every college and university leader must strive for trust. If trust is achieved, every situation will be successfully led and managed.

Effective communication is essential. All stakeholders need to be aware of what they are expected to do and why during crises.

PK-12 SCHOOLS—JODI LAMB AND FERN AEFSKY

In the next section of this chapter, practitioners shared various questions that they think need to be addressed by leadership during crisis management. At the beginning of each subsection, the questions will be listed and then discussed.

Financial Implications

Questions

If there is a significant budget shortfall, how can our schools and districts do more with less?

Are there plans in place so that monies available can be used flexibly?

As the pandemic unfolded in the spring of 2020, the leaders of the federal department of education for the United States provided ongoing guidance of how both state educational agencies (SEAs) and local educational agencies (LEAs) could receive flexibility on many aspects of federal funding. This response was prompted by the authorization of the Coronavirus Aid, Relief, and Economic Security (CARES) Act.

This flexibility meant that K-12 districts could do things like distribute laptops, previously designated for a different purpose, to students for virtual learning through the use of funding from the Elementary and Secondary School Education Relief or ESSER fund (U.S. Department of Education, April 23, 2020). It meant that funding could be shifted for different purposes with an expedited approval process. The flexibility provided at the federal level meant district and school leaders could more creatively address the needs of students as they moved into weeks of virtual learning (U.S. Department of Education, April 29, 2020).

Federal monies through IDEA also offered some flexibility as demonstrated by the IDEA guidance document provided (U.S. Department of Education, June 25, 2020). This report stated that states could set aside funds for other activities at the state level that may be necessary as a result of the pandemic. Examples provided include technology with UDL principle, assistive technology, and building capacity activities. All measures support services for children with disabilities.

Career and technical programs were afforded the option of being able to donate personal protective equipment (PPE) that had been purchased for the 2019–2020 school year to local public hospitals (U.S. Department of Education, April 14, 2020). These initiatives eased the burden that school and district leaders were facing as they guided their organizations into virtual instruction and tried hard to make education accessible to all students. Both Kentucky and Texas reported (Marsee, 2020; Texas Education Agency, 2020) that at least 90 percent of the funding that the state received for education through the CARES Act will be sent to districts.

Superintendents received guidance on flexibility available through both state and federal sources to meet the challenges of educating children during a pandemic.

> Many questions about MOE can be answered with a plain read of section 18008 of the CARES Act, reprinted below for convenience: MAINTENANCE OF EFFORT SEC. 18008. (a) A State's application for funds to carry out sections 18002 or 18003 of this title shall include assurances that the State will maintain support for elementary and secondary education, and State support for higher education (which shall include State funding to institutions of higher education and state need-based financial aid, and shall not include support for capital projects or for research and development or tuition and fees paid by students) in fiscal years 2020 and 2021 at least at the levels of such support that is the average of such State's support for elementary and secondary education and

for higher education provided in the 3 fiscal years preceding the date of enactment of this Act. (b) The secretary may waive the requirement in subsection (a) for the purpose of relieving fiscal burdens on States that have experienced a precipitous decline in financial resources. (USDOE, May 2020, p. ii)

State and local leaders braced for a future of financial uncertainty. With the economic impact of sheltering in place and massive unemployment, the 2020–2021 and the 2021–2022 state budget forecasts look grim. Many states predicted a multibillion-dollar shortfall (Burnette, 2020). States that relied on funding from sources like luxury taxes and sales taxes were significantly impacted with the shelter-in-place order.

The shortfall of income due to most businesses being shut down for eight to twelve weeks on top of record-breaking unemployment benefits being paid out is enough to put most states on the edge of economic shutdown. For example, Hawaii is predicting a $1.5 billion shortfall due to the fact that the budget is primarily based on tourism (Burnette, 2020). As of June 2020, Idaho reduced the 2020–2021 K-12 state budget by $99 million (Morton, 2020) with more cuts anticipated.

Additionally, due to high amounts of state and federal aid getting paid out during the pandemic for other social supports, both federal and state aid were cut significantly for the 2020–2021 school year and/or the 2021–2022. Districts that rely heavily on that aid will be impacted considerably. The lasting impact on districts already concerned about significant cuts could be significant.

The American Association of School Administrators (AASA) reported in the *U.S. News* that $245 billion would be needed to reopen schools safely, across the United States (Camera, 2020). This national organization estimated needs based on costs aligned with operating virtually and face-to face instruction, addressing students' learning gaps resulting from academic losses from March 2020 to June 2020, and losses in state and local funding due to reductions in funding sources due to a loss of tax revenues.

School districts leaders have to reevaluate that current resources will need to cover multiple forms of instructions, technology for virtual activities, and personnel costs in a changing learning environment. As costs increase, aid decreases, and layers of instructional opportunities for administrators, teachers, staff, and students multiply; leaders need to garner support and assistance from stakeholders and partnerships.

Facilities and School Safety

Questions

How can we open school and provide for safe, social distancing?
How will that impact class size?

If making classes smaller is the chosen option, where do I find enough teachers to hire, will there be funding for salaries, and how can I safely create additional classroom space?

If my school was built for smaller class sizes and has small rooms, how can I create enough space between students to keep everyone safe?

What do we do about programs such as athletics and band?

How do we handle lunches?

How do we handle hallway space as well as arrival and dismissal procedures?

As mentioned in the previous section, state guidelines were provided to districts. These guidelines were drawn from ones provided federally. The U.S. Department of Education, in collaboration with the Centers for Disease Control and Prevention (CDC), provided guidance for schools (CDC, May 19, 2020). The guidance is based upon current social distancing and other safety practices that are related to the COVID pandemic. Each recommendation, while doable, creates another set of challenges.

For example, the CDC (2020) recommended having students bring their own lunches and eat in classrooms. One challenge will be for those who are on free or reduced-price lunch. Conceivably, each child could receive a bag lunch or a plated meal, but there will be additional costs of disposable trays or bags. A second challenge will relate to lunch supervision.

Many teacher contracts call for a duty-free lunch. If that was the case, how can the students eat in the classrooms and be supervised properly while teachers are relieved to each their own lunch? A third challenge was for secondary school schedules, as not all students and teachers are scheduled for the same lunch, so finding rooms available for lunch was a significant challenge.

A second example relates to classroom arrangements. The CDC (2020) recommended that all desks face forward and students are kept six feet apart whenever possible. From a facility perspective, for most schools, the only way to accomplish this is to cut the students in each class in half. How can this work using the pre-pandemic model? The answer is that it cannot. Not only did schools need to consider alternative schedules, they needed to consider the impact on expected instructional strategies and the use of instructional materials since the CDC recommended that toys, manipulatives, and texts be not used by multiple children.

This guideline raised more questions such as "Do we have enough materials so that each student can have their own set?" "Do we need to amend the teacher observation instruments to represent teaching during the pandemic v. teaching prior to the pandemic?"

According to Superville (2020), this was the perfect time for districts to examine the possibility of year-round schedules. This model was tried by many and is currently in use in a small number of schools/districts nationally. Primarily, while there are many benefits to this schedule, its lack of popularity with communities and parents has been a primary downfall. Now, in the midst of a pandemic, this model provided flexibility districts and schools were looking for while providing parents a way to get back to work.

Technology

Specific information about issues with technology, such as the digital dive many people were faced with around the country, was discussed in previous chapters. The need of leaders to manage technology issues is what will be discussed in this section.

Questions

If the country has to go back to virtual education for long term, how can we obtain enough devices and Internet to support students and their families?

For the schools and districts that handed out devices for families who had none, what percentage did not return the devices? What policies should be implemented to protect the district or school from loss?

Will the definition of a "school day" need to change? What leniency will be given at the state and federal levels?

In light of the widely publicized grading issues during the spring transition to virtual, can schools accurately measure student growth in an uncontrolled virtual setting?

How can districts and schools support families where both parents need to work (therefore needing students to attend school)?

Virtual education solves many of the issues identified in the previous section. However, it also has some complicating factors. If children need to be educated virtually, that means an adult must stay at home. At the same time, there are some benefits to the forced transition to virtual as a result of the pandemic. Gabrieli and Beaudoin (2020) suggested that this experience might just be the impetus that the profession needed to break away from outdated learning structures.

For example, they suggested that virtual education, along with a traditional face-to-face setting, provided additional opportunities for extended learning and greater collaboration of teachers and students. Perhaps there is a blend of the two approaches that might, in the end, make a much stronger instructional model.

Technology use through virtual education was one way that helped with required social distancing measures. For example, several universities looked at alternative schedules where half the students attend class one day and the other half access the class via Zoom. For the next class meeting, the groups switch so that every student meets face-to-face with the professors every other class meeting. It is possible for a similar schedule to work for high school students. Another idea that was posed was a conversion of the cafeteria and gymnasiums or multipurpose rooms into oversized computer labs where students could be engaged in virtual instruction and supervised by paraprofessionals or other staff members.

Embracing virtual education as a viable option is a smart way to keep more students engaged whether the interruption to traditional school setting is due to any crisis. Educational leaders have identified multiple variables to ensure equal access for educational services. This occurred during the pandemic, school shootings and safety situations, and weather-related closures (hurricanes, blizzards, tornados). Leadership team members must be prepared to delegate and manage multiple aspects of any crisis.

Transportation

Questions

How should bus routes be adjusted to practice social distancing and how do we add more drivers and buses?

How can we ensure social distancing and sanitization on the buses?

If athletics and music competitions continue, how does this impact scheduling?

Hannon (2020) reported on a webinar held in May by Transfinder. Districts and states are reporting that while it will be important to follow social distancing guidelines for buses, that virtual education may actually alleviate some of the burden of finding ways to make that possible. Many parents opted for virtual education for their children. Keeping students at home reduced the strain on the transportation system.

Some districts asked parents to register their children for transportation services so that the district can safely assign buses and drivers to the routes. Morton (2020) reported that some states issued very specific guidelines. Colorado required that bus routes be reduced to twenty students from the typical seventy-seven students and all drivers will be required to wear masks.

There was a concern that this pandemic may actually exacerbate the driver shortage that many districts report. After school shootings, often bus drivers resign, due to fear and no plan to ensure safety on buses. Hannon (2020) indicated that many drivers are considered at-risk as it relates to COVID-19 due to either age or health conditions. According to Morton (2020), over 40 percent of drivers in Oregon are in the at-risk category. If those drivers decide to not return, superintendents will be faced with hiring new drivers. However, since many departments of motor vehicles and highway safety have remained closed, new drivers were not able to get trained and obtain the commercial driver license required for bus operations.

Human Resources

Questions

What changes in the contract would be necessary to allow for more scheduling flexibility?

How does the teacher work day need to be defined to accommodate for flexible scheduling?

If the state/district experienced a financial shortfall and budget cuts ensue, how will teacher morale impact contract negotiations?

How will the districts mandate required absences (should a COVID-19 outbreak occur)?

How will teachers be compensated?

If an outbreak occurs in one classroom and everyone from that room is put on quarantine, will the teacher be expected to provide instruction?

For public school districts that participate in the state retirement system, should teachers be categorized as frontline workers and therefore receive benefits at a level comparable with law enforcement?

During a crisis, items covered in the teachers and/or administrators' contracts may not be implementable. Leaders need the flexibility to make exceptions based on priorities during a crisis. Depending on the district and state, teacher contracts typically contain language that outlines an agreed-upon work day, professional responsibilities, accrual of sick and personal time, evaluation time frames, and other benefits.

Another area to consider addressing is teacher evaluations. Do the observation tools need to be different to address the differences in instruction? Maintaining valid and accurate records is critical and providing helpful feedback supports strong teacher reflection. Additionally, for administrators who worked all year to support and/or documented a struggling teacher, what happened to that consistency once the pandemic hit? How does professional coaching and mentoring look different when we are using virtual education?

Mental Health Services

In an earlier chapter, information regarding mental health needs of all stakeholders during crises was presented. This section raises additional considerations of concern by school and district administrators.

Questions

Should the district consider adding additional counselors and therapists to address the greater need?

Is it anticipated that new rules regarding sufficient mental health services will be produced at the state or federal level?

What practices should administrators have in place to be sure administrators feel support and are encouraged to do the same for their faculty and staff?

The interconnectedness of human resources, finances, and personnel must be considered in collaboration of many during crisis management. How resources are allocated, by whom and for whom, and how to meet needs of new mandates resulting from the crisis at hand all provide leaders with challenges. For example, being told to have more personnel available so that lunch breaks can be provided works well if you have funds to hire more personnel. Often, the mandate is given by the state or federal governments, but no monies are given. At the local level, the leaders have to cut other services to then meet that mandate.

Professionals who provide mental health support are often cut, as those services are not mandated by education law. However, in times of crisis those services are desperately needed. Suggestions are made to coordinate and collaborate with service providers in the community, but many communities have a shortage of those support personnel as well.

A group of aspiring administrators were asked to provide information about the transition to virtual education and the lessons they and their administrators had learned during the transition. One teacher summed it up best when asked what her administration could do to provide support to her:

> This question overwhelms me. My initial answer was everything . . . but that is not realistic. As I write this, I currently have 120 different missing assignments from any number of my 155 students. During out team meeting this past Tuesday, my team expressed our stress level to my principal and she helped us in attempting to put an end to some of our stress. We made a decision that we will take late work for a period of time, but after 2 weeks—we can no longer manage it. We expressed to my principal that we respect giving students grace and to monitor their stress level but we explained—what about our stress level? She mentioned that this topic is coming up a lot that the principals' meetings. (A. Danisovsky, personal communication, May 2, 2020)

In a webinar provided by the Association for Supervision and Curriculum Development (ASCD), Pejavara and Slade (June 2, 2020) recommended that schools and districts look closely that the trauma-informed care model as back-to-school plans are developed. Schools that integrate social-emotional learning can address student issues through this process.

It is important for school and district administrators to develop protocols for supporting each other while they attend to teacher and student stress. As reported by Tate (2020), leadership personnel should pay attention to the social-emotional competencies from both the top-down and the bottom-up. A system must be in place that concentrates on everyone's psychosocial health and well-being. As was suggested at the beginning of this chapter, schools, districts, and states must have crisis plans in place that address issues of mental health. These programs will help to better serve students as they struggle with elements dealing with a crisis.

OPENING OF PK-12 SCHOOLS—ED DADEZ

Dr. Anthony Fauci, the nation's chief epidemiologist, and other federal health officials reported to the U.S. Senate Health, Education, Labor, and Pensions Committee that "[w]ithout a vaccine to halt the spread of the coronavirus, widespread testing and tracing of the illness will be essential to ensure public confidence that children can safely return to school in the fall" (Blad, 2020). Cliff Young, president of Ipsos, stated that "[a]s our world has changed, almost everything we do has changed, including how we view and approach education. Though Americans were optimistic about a return to in-person learning, there was angst among teachers, parents, and America at large about how to keep our schools safe if the virus isn't fully contained" (Page, 2020).

It is critically important that PK-12 school leadership personnel determine the most effective and efficient means to persuade teachers and staff to return to the schools; assuage the hesitancies of parents; successfully apply social distancing; and implement (or continue) virtual learning strategies.

Randi Weingarten, president of the American Federation of Teachers (AFT), one of the two largest teachers' unions in the country, stated that they "will encourage its affiliates to lobby districts for five conditions before opening schools: a decline in cases over 14 days; adequate testing, tracing and isolation; public health measures like temperature taking, cleaning protocols, personal protective equipment and physical distancing measures such as staggered school times; transparency and fidelity to safety measures and enforcement; and increased funding to implement the host of changes" (Gaudiano, 2020). In addition, AFT's affiliate in New York City, United Federation of

Teachers, has called for widespread testing, temperature checks, rigorous cleaning, and protective gear in every school as well as exhaustive tracing procedures as conditions for reopening schools.

Another issue as it pertains to reopening schools were school administrators, teachers, and staff who had compromised immune systems based on hypertension, asthma, obesity, heart disease, cancer, diabetes, and so on. Somewhere between 20 and 35 percent of the teaching workforce were fifty years old or older and may live in multigenerational households with family members who are also high risk. AFT has also recommended "educators with high-risk for severe infections remain at home and teach remotely via video to students who are physically in the classroom and overseen by staff" (Camera, 2020). There was a belief that many teachers will choose to retire or resign, rather than go back into classrooms.

"Since children and young adults can be asymptomatic reopening schools would put everyone from teachers and administrators to lunch workers and guidance counselors at risk for COVID-19" (Hinebaugh & Sheridan, 2020). The transmission of the virus included the possibility of bringing it home to parents and families. Additionally, pediatric inflammatory multisystem syndrome may be more lethal than we thought for those under the age of eighteen. Reynolds (2020) reported that "[m]ost cases of COVID-19 in children are mild, but studies suggest kids may play a major role in transmitting the virus to each other and to vulnerable adults—and that keeping schools closed for longer may help stop the spread of coronavirus."

The majority of school districts were closed through the spring of 2020 and parents struggled with childcare and employment, if they were able to work, because of COVID-19. With hopefully everyone back to work by the fall, what will parents do if their child is still at home? Reopening schools is an issue that needs to be overcome, but "[u]nless plans are thoughtful and nearly foolproof, parents won't be comfortable putting their children—and themselves—at risk" (Sherman, 2020).

Forty percent of teachers and parents believe schools should not reopen until there is a coronavirus vaccine. Seventy percent of parents want their child to wear a mask while at school. Sixty-six percent say their child would find it hard to comply with social distancing (Page, 2020). Similar to teachers, parents and families do not feel comfortable sending their child back to school unless they feel their child will be safe. The feeling is that parents are concerned that their child or other children will most likely not adhere to proper hygiene, good handwashing, wearing masks, and social distancing and then bring COVID-19 home to other family members.

One way to provide social distancing is to have less students at schools. School districts examined options of this type, including not opening, opening completely, or a hybrid method. Strauss (2020) reported that "[m]any districts have said they are considering having students in on some school days but not others so that social distancing rules inside classrooms can be respected." Other means of this occurring could be rotating schedules with some of your classmates at home and some in the classroom; staggered starts, with some grades or cohorts starting early morning and others starting after lunch; and some days your grade is at school while other grades are at home taking virtual classes. Sixty percent of parents and teachers endorsed returning to schools for two to three days a week and utilizing virtual learning the other days (Page, 2020).

Ninety percent of teachers surveyed said it would be nearly impossible to enforce having students comply with social distancing (Page, 2020). PK-5 students would find it very difficult to understand the importance of social distancing. Some believe it would be better to have only middle and high school students returning in the fall.

Krouse (2020) reported that Jason Farley, professor and nurse epidemiologist at Johns Hopkins University School of Nursing in Maryland, stated that "[t]eachers should be thinking about managing the physical environment as much as they're managing the learning environment," which would include social distancing and cleanliness. There will be a need for additional staff to assist with the safety of students.

Compounding the issue of reopening schools was the certainty of state and local governments cutting education budgets at a time when budgets needed to be increased. Strauss (2020) stated that recent *Washington Post* polls "taken of K-12 teachers and the other of parents with school-age children found that 73 percent of parents and 64 percent of teachers said they believe that children will eventually make up for learning lost because of the disruption of school during the coronavirus crisis." These were good percentages but not great numbers. Much will need to be done to ensure this percentage is met and surpassed.

It is important for all educational administrators and teachers to remember that effective leaders build and maintain a safe, caring, and healthy school environment that meets the academic, social, emotional, and physical needs of each student. Parents and community stakeholders want to be assured that their children will be safe in schools. Educational leaders need to do all that can be done to manage schools safely and well, as guarantees cannot be made.

SUMMARY

Issues facing leaders of all P-20 institutions are similar, as the needs of students are the priority, closely followed by their parents, faculty, and staff working with the school, college, and/or university community. Loss of revenue, gaps in learning, measurements of learning (tests and grades), health and safety issues, and long-term, short-term, and immediate needs all contribute to significant challenges and decisions that need to be made by institutional leaders.

Geographical location matters, as communities have different priorities at various times. Hurricanes and other weather-related events (blizzards, ice storms, flooding), health crises (SARS, H1N1, COVID-19, local outbreaks of measles, meningitis), and safety issues (school shootings, car accidents, violence, suicide) are all events where leaders have to lead others through crises.

Most importantly, student need to be able to learn and demonstrate knowledge. When crises require changes in practice, leaders must continue to identify needs, implement change, and facilitate people and policies that help students achieve learning outcomes in a safe manner.

REFERENCES

Bacevice, Peter. (2020, June 25). Are students ready to return to campus in the fall? *University Business*.

Blad, E. (2020, May 12). COVID-19 Testing Key to Reopening Schools, Health Officials Tell Senators. *Education Week*. https://www.edweek.org/education/covid-19-testing-key-to-reopening-schools-health-officials-tell-senators/2020/05.

Burnette, D. (2020, May 13). School districts are on the brink. *Education Week*, pp. 12–13.

Camera, L. (2020, June 24). Schools need $245 billion to reopen safely, state education chiefs estimate. *U.S. News Report*.

Cohen, P., & Casselman, B. (2020, June 6). For laid-off minorities, recovery looks distant. *New York Times*. https://link-gale-com.saintleo.idm.oclc.org/apps/doc/A625839688/HCRA?

Florida Department of Education. (2020, June 11). Governor Ron DeSantis announces recommendations to safely reopen Florida's education system. [Press release]. http://www.fldoe.org/newsroom/latest-news/governor-ron-desantis-announces-recommendations-to-safely-reopen-floridas-education-system.stml.

Florida Department of Education. (2020, June 24). Governor Ron DeSantis signs historic teacher pay increases into law [Press release]. http://www.fldoe.org/newsroom/latest-news/governor-ron-desantis-signs-historic-teacher-pay-increases-into-law.stml.

Gabrieli, C., & Beaudoin, C. (2020, June). In a time of crisis, what can we learn about learning time? *Educational Leadership*, 77, 12–18.

Gaudiano, Nicole. (2020, April 28). Teachers union: "Scream Bloody Murder" if schools reopen against medical advice. *Politico*. https://www.politico.com/news/2020/04/28/teachers-unions-consider-strikes-protests-if-schools-reopen-against-medical-advice-215210.

Gurel, E., & Tat, M. (2017). SWOT Analysis: A Theoretical Review. *Journal of International Social Research* 10(51), 994–1006. https://doi.org/10.17719/jisr.2017.1832.

Hannon, T. (2020, May 7). What happens to school transportation when the COVID-19 dust settles? *School Transportation News*. https://stnonline.com/news/what-happens-to-school-transportation-when-the-covid-19-dust-settles/.

Hinebaugh, J., & Sheridan, K. (2020, April 16). Should Florida schools reopen in May? Parents and teachers say no. *WUSF News*. https://wusfnews.wusf.usf.edu/education/2020-04-16/should-florida-schools-reopen-in-may-parents-and-teachers-say-no.

Inside Higher Education Staff. (2020, July 7). COVID-9 roundup: More universities announce online plans. *Inside Higher Education*.

Jaycox, L., Tanielian, T., Sharma, P., Morse, L., Clum, G., & Stein, B. (2007). Schools' mental health responses after hurricanes Katrina and Rita. *Psychiatric Services*, *58*(10), 1339–43.

Lederman, Doug. (2020, June 29). College president increasingly worried about perceived value of degrees. *Inside Higher Education*.

Marsee, M. (2020). Kentucky schools could receive more than 200 million in federal COVID19 relief funds. https://www.kentuckyteacher.org/news/2020/04/kentucky-schools-could-receive-more-than-200m-in-federal-covid-19-relief-funds/.

McCauley, M., Minsky, S., & Viswanath, K. (2013, December 3). The H1N1 pandemic: Media frames, stigmatization, and coping. *BMC Public Health*. doi: http://dx.doi.org.saintleo.idm.oclc.org/10.1186/1471-2458-13-1116.

Morton, N. (2020, June 24). Who will drive school buses during the pandemic? *High Country News*. https://www.hcn.org/articles/covid19-who-will-drive-school-buses-during-the-pandemic.

Page, S. (2020, May 26). Back to school? 1 in 5 teachers are unlikely to return to reopened classrooms this fall, poll says. *USA Today*. https://www.usatoday.com/story/news/education/2020/05/26/coronavirus-schools-teachers-poll-ipsos-parents-fall-online/5254729002/.

Pejavara, A., & Slade, S. (2020, June 2). Leading schools during the coronavirus crisis: Planning for reopening. *Association for Supervision and Curriculum Development*.

Reynolds, E. (2020, May 6). Should your kids go back to school? These studies suggest not. *CNN Health*. https://www.click2houston.com/news/local/2020/05/06/should-your-kids-go-back-to-school-these-studies-suggest-not/.

Rosenberg, Brian. (2020, July 7). The cruelty of ICE's guidance for international students. *The Chronicle of Higher Education*.

Sarker, P., & Lester, H. (2019, May 29). Post-disaster recovery associations of power systems dependent critical infrastructures. *Infrastructures*.

Sherman, A. (2020, May 5). Will schools be open in September? We asked several experts to weigh in. *CNBC Digital Series: The Next Normal*. https://www.cnbc.com/2020/05/04/will-schools-be-open-in-september-experts-weigh-in.html.

Strauss, V. (2020, May 26). Polls: 20 percent of teachers not like to return to classrooms if schools reopen in the fall. *The Washington Post*. https://www.washingtonpost.com/education/2020/05/26/polls-20-percent-teachers-not-likely-return-classrooms-if-schools-reopen-this-fall/.

Superville, D. (2020, June 24). Is it time to reconsider the year-round school schedule? *Education Week.* http://www.edweek.org/ew/articles/2020/06/25/is-it-time-to-consider-the-year-round.html.

Tate, E. (2020, May 7). Why social-emotional learning is suddenly in the spotlight. *EdSurge.* https://www.edsurge.com/news/2019-05-07-why-social-emotional-learning-is-suddenly-in-the-spotlight.

Texas Education Agency. (2020). https://tea.texas.gov/texas-schools/health-safety-discipline/covid/covid-19-support-texas-educators.

U.S. Department of Education. (2020, April 14). Secretary DeVos announces CTE programs can donate unused personal protective equipment, medical supplies to support coronavirus response [Press release]. https://www.ed.gov/news/press-releases/secretary-devos-announces-cte-programs-can-donate-unused-personal-protective-equipment-medical-supplies-support-coronavirus-response.

U.S. Department of Education. (2020, April 23). Secretary DeVos makes available over $13 billion in emergency coronavirus relief to support continued education for K-12 students [Press release]. https://www.ed.gov/news/press-releases/secretary-devos-makes-available-over-13-billion-emergency-coronavirus-relief-support-continued-education-k-12-students.

U.S. Department of Education. (2020, April 29). Fact sheet for repurposing federal equipment and supplies to combat COVID-19 [Fact sheet]. https://www2.ed.gov/documents/coronavirus/covid19-repurposing-equipment-supplies.pdf.

U.S. Department of Education. (2020, May). Frequently asked questions on the maintenance-of-effort requirements applicable to the CARES act programs.

U.S. Department of Education. (2020, June 25). QA use of funds, Part B. https://www2.ed.gov/policy/speced/guid/idea/memosdcltrs/qa-part-b-use-of-funds-06-25-2020.pdf.

Zalaznick, Matt. (2020, June 22). Why managing risk—and panic—is key to keeping colleges open. *University Business.*

Chapter 8

Crisis Leadership: Lessons Learned

Fern Aefsky

Principles and critical components of effective crisis leadership entail active communication, leading decisively, flexibility, resiliency, trust, transparency, adaptability, and empathy (Gigliotti, 2017; Nichols et al., 2020). When crises occur, they test the skills, knowledge, and abilities of leaders to guide others through unanticipated and unexpected events.

There are different types of crises, those that can be expected and planned for and those that are emergencies that are unexpected, atypical, and very unusual. Examples of those that can be planned for include weather-related emergencies (hurricanes, blizzards, flooding, shelters), school safety plans, and personnel shortages. Unanticipated emergencies examples include domestic terrorism (9/11/01 events), national disasters, and pandemic.

These crises impact society, and the impact on P-20 schools is significant. Leadership competencies for various educational positions have been identified with key competencies of vision, integrity, content knowledge, confidence, decision-making, and an understanding of organizational systems, problem-solving, operational management, and commitment (Litz, 2011).

Leadership transcends across cultures. In various countries across the globe, leaders build and sustain relationships, increase team capacity, recognize the values and structures of organizations, and focus on goal and mission alignment and purpose. All are critical aspects of leadership development.

Petrigleri (2020) identified attributes of effective crisis leadership. He suggested the psychological definition of "holding," which describes how a person in an authority role understands and communicates what is happening when a crisis occurs. This enables others to feel less stress, with recognition that someone is in as much control of a situation as possible and will lead others through the crisis.

Values and ethics of leadership define the interactions between leaders and those they influence (Aefsky, 2017). If a culture of the organization supports trust, relationships, and transparency in a positive way, and the leader is a transformational leader prior to a crisis, the leader's ability to manage through the crisis is greatly enhanced.

Educational leaders have dealt with the issues and aftermaths of school safety and school as a result of the numerous school shootings, injuries, and deaths caused by multiple events in the United States and globally. Implementation of techniques, strategies, and plans assisted school district personnel, families, and students in being prepared.

However, nothing prepared educators for the pandemic of 2020 that caused schools to close quickly, move to a virtual teaching and learning environment for all, in a matter of weeks.

As discussed in previous chapters, leaders had to adapt quickly and help others do the same. Numerous challenges occurred, from teacher, administrator, staff, family, and community stakeholders.

Attributes of good leadership evolves from points of ethical leadership theories and practice. Organizational leaders can impact decision making and the ethical behaviors of employees by viewing opportunities through the lens of ethical leadership protocols (Al Halbusi et al., 2019; Chikeleze & Baehrend, 2017). When leaders model ethical behaviors throughout a crisis, engagement of others increases, as does trust of the leader (Engelbrecht et al., 2014).

Researchers have identified critical components to effective crisis leadership skills, which are similar to the identified attributes of ethical leadership (Gigliotti, 2017; Nichols et al., 2020; Vukajlovic et al., 2019). Priorities need to be identified, and there must be flexibility as priorities change based on information that may change suddenly and frequently. Establishing a system, leadership teams to address issues as they arise and be able to make quick decisions are important components for leaders to implement.

Identification of people, their roles and responsibilities related to the crisis, and communication of any changes as they occur are critical. Communication speed, transparency, and accuracy matter. In crises involving school shootings, rumors and misinformation occur and clarity of facts helps leaders manage the ensuing chaos. This occurs not just during the event but also in the aftermath and in preparation for pro-active measures for potential future threats and events. Social media tends to fuel much misinformation.

During the COVID-19 pandemic, these same leadership systems needed to be in place. Crises can vary, and some variables may differ, but at the core, the systemic approaches and parameters are the same. Educational leaders need to try to be in front of changing circumstances, and discussions with crisis teams have to focus on immediate, short-term, and long-term activities and plans. Communication of what is and is not going to happen based on facts at hand is important, with the caveat that if data changes, so may those plans of action.

Leaders need to take care of their constituents. Those constituents include their clients (students, faculty, staff, families) and their leadership teams. Leaders during a crisis need to do "welfare checks" on their stakeholders, and a plan must be in place to ensure consistency of those checks. People are isolated during crises for a variety of reasons, and that isolation can contribute to misinformation being shared, anxiousness by stakeholders regarding other stakeholders, and a resistance to asking for help if needed.

Murthy (2020) described the paradox of situational loneliness as an indicator of people withdrawing from others, and they do not know how to engage during a crisis. Many people feel that others need more assistance or that they do not want to bother people, which contributes to anxiety for themselves. If leaders reach out, people are more likely to feel supported and able to ask questions, be supportive, and get support as needed.

Here are some student, parent, teacher, and administrator experiences that they wanted to share of social impact and needs during the pandemic in 2020.

SOCIAL IMPACT

Logan, High School Senior—Florida

The social impact of distance learning and quarantine in general was the most significant change in my life. Like many of my peers, I initially felt crushed that I might never get to see some of my favorite teachers or best friends ever again and that I would miss out on my senior prom, GradBash, and other senior year festivities. I worked hard and pushed myself to excel in school since I was a little kid, so to miss out on these celebrations that I had been looking forward to for such a long time felt like a real slap in the face.

However, since we live in the age of technology, I was easily able to stay in contact with my friends, and I had access to my teachers. Moreover, I am incredibly grateful for the efforts of the community to celebrate us as seniors through events such as graduation parades and the Adopt a Senior Facebook group. I am eternally an optimist, so these efforts helped turn what was initially a heartbreaking end to my senior year into a valuable and heartwarming experience.

Parent of Two High School Students—New York

We lived in a small town outside of Albany. Our graduation class was under 200. I didn't have any difficulty with cooperation of teacher or district during this crisis. My son had an extremely hard time with remote learning. He is more of a visual learner and needs to be in a classroom. He struggled learning the information on his own and refused to reach out for help.

This whole thing would have been more depressing for him had the farm he works at not offered him hours to work. He was able to do his schoolwork and get out of the house and go to work. My daughter cooperated with everything she was asked to do. However, we were very concerned with her stress level and depression of being away from her friends.

Grandparents—Florida/Maryland

In the grand scheme of this pandemic, the lack of socialization, physical contact, physical activity, limited online schooling instruction, and parental work demands spilled over to affect some grandparents as well. The unusual aspect of this was the fact that we live hundreds of miles away.

In an effort to maintain family contact and acclimate to the changing dynamic of home/work/school demands, we were inundated with FaceTime calls, Hangout calls, and emails. Not from our middle-aged children, but from their offspring aged four through nine.

This occurred multiple times a day, every day. They craved the unique contact this method of socializing provided. And, honestly, we craved it too. The parents, being so overwhelmed by working from home, feeling unproductive, unfulfilled, and stressed, gave way to the newest venue of virtual home childcare, namely grandma and grandpa. After a couple of months of silly, repetitive content, we instituted structure into our multiple calls.

Teacher—California

From a classroom management standpoint, the online model totally eliminated behavior issues. Once we set the ground rules for our online class, everyone was well behaved. It was pleasant to not have to write any referrals. I cannot remember the last time I had this long a stretch without butting heads with students.

Second Teacher—California

I noticed some of my students who normally are average or poor learners excelled with the digital methodologies. The group I saw the most improvement from were students who are the quiet, shy ones and the ones who have anxiety.

Administrator—Florida

The isolation was significant when we started virtually meeting to discuss reopening of schools. The lack of having an emotional break over the summer negatively impacted everyone's ability to be motivated and engaged to start a new year with so many questions about health and safety unanswered.

SUMMARY

Leaders needed to deal with consideration of the mental health issues of all stakeholders in a caring and proactive manner. Resources needed to be allocated for a cadre of assessment, intervention, and support.

Politicians and government officials must pay attention to the needs of students, personnel, and school districts when allocating funds for education. Every state had standards in their departments of education that mention students need to be educated in a safe learning environment.

The economic impact of traumas in schools results in a reallocation of funding. When school shootings occurred, there was a national movement and state requirements to increase school resource officers and/or police presence in schools. However, funding did not increase to cover the local costs, by either states or national government. If funding appeared to be increased, it was due to a loss of funding in another area of education so that the bottom line did not adequately increase and leaders had to make difficult choices in order to meet new mandates.

The Framework for Safe and Successful Schools (2013) report suggested that school principals and district leaders must be able to use financial resources to best meet the needs of individual schools' students and community; engage collaborative partnerships for support; and improve access to mental health services (Cowan et al., 2013). While these were initially offered as a result of school shooting traumas, they are appropriate considerations for any crises management situations.

Leaders were faced with a continuing evolving crisis as plans for reopening schools after the 2020 pandemic needed to occur. National and state officials, politicians, and medical experts were not in agreement with guidance and plans for reopening schools after the five- to six-month closures.

Educators were concerned about health and safety due to the pandemic. However, leaders needed to concern themselves with all other aspects of education at the PK-20 levels. Enrollment, academic achievement, learning gaps, personnel, and issues of social justice are a few of the main concerns shared by parents, students, teachers, administrators, staff, and community stakeholders.

Facilitating a cycle of continued progress is the role of leaders of all schools, colleges, and universities. Recognition and acceptance that a new normal would likely be established assisted those in leadership roles in their journeys to get their organizations through the next number of months successfully, while getting to their new normal. Finances, materials for teaching and learning, teacher training, flexibility with state tests, entrance exams, and being flexible with virtual options are all possibilities that have to be planned for effectively.

The existence of many organizations, inclusive of businesses and schools, is economically challenged and some institutions will not survive. Unexpected crises threaten organizations, and leaders need to be prepared to move their organizations forward (Woo, 2015).

Planning for strategic risks is a major consideration of leaders dealing with crises management (Smith, 2014). The ability to respond in real time, consistently and with confidence, alleviates fear and anxiety in those being led. Leaders need to have the insight and instinct to move things forward in unchartered territory, as crises are unexpected, novel, and vary in scope.

Using the framework of SWOT analyses offers leaders a concrete framework from which to move forward in times of crises management. Doing a SWOT analysis is one way to assess, reassess, and lead forward. Identify the strengths, weaknesses, opportunities, and threats (SWOT) is a method to assist leaders in making good organizational decisions (Schooley, 2019). This technique can be useful in framing out issues in a macro and micro manner.

Collaboration is very important during crises management. Leaders should work with other leaders to get the support they need to keep going, as leaders need to be able to digest, invest, and model behaviors that support the organization and all stakeholders. It is not an easy task to lead as tragedies occur. There is an emotional toll on leaders that need to be recognized and supported. Working together helps everyone get through the crises events and allows recognition of accountability, success, and challenges that are faced together.

Prior to the COVID pandemic that impacted all schools, colleges, and universities in 2020, there was not a single crisis that impacted the whole country or world in a similar fashion. The lessons learned are applicable to every crisis situation and should be remembered.

While everyone believed this type of trauma will not occur again in our collective lifetimes, it was predicted that recovery to schools would be a three- to five-year process to establish a new normal. During that projected time, there will be other traumas that leaders will be called upon to deal with in individual schools or districts. We need to remember why communication, flexibility, transparency, and collaboration matter.

REFERENCES

Aefsky, F. (2017). *Collaborative leadership: Building capacity through effective partnerships*. Rowman & Littlefield.

Al Halbusi, H., Ismail, M., & Omar, S. (May 2019). Examining the impact of ethical leadership on employees ethical behavior. *Journal of Technology Management and Business, 6*(2), 389–98.

Chikeleze, M., & Baehrend, W. (2017). Ethical leadership and its impact on decision making. *Journal of Leadership Studies, 11*(2), 45–47.

Cowan, K. C., Vaillancourt, K., Rossen, E., & Pollitt, K. (2013). *A framework for safe and successful schools* [Brief]. National Association of School Psychologists.

Engelbrecht, A., Heine, G., & Mahembe, B. (2014). *The influence of ethical leadership on trust and work engagement. SA Journal of Industrial Psychology, 40*(1).

Gigliotti, R. (May 2017). 6 critical components of effective crisis leadership. *ICMA*.

Litz, D. (August 2011). Globalization and the changing face of educational leadership: Current trends and emerging dilemmas. *International Education Studies, 4*(3). Published by Canadian Center of Science and Education 47.

Murthy, V. (2020). *Together: The healing power of human connection in a sometimes lonely world*. HarperCollins.

Nichols, C., Hayden, S., & Trendler, C. (2020, April 2). 4 behaviors that help leaders manage a crisis. *Harvard Business Review*.

Petriglieri, G. (2020, April 22). *The psychology behind effective crisis leadership*. Harvard Business Publishing.

Schooley, S. (2019, June 23). SWOT analysis: What it is and when to use it. *Business News Daily*.

Smith, J. (2014). Crisis management: Preparing for the next big event. *Deloitte*. http://www.deloitte.com.

Vukajlovic, V., Simeunovic, I., Beraha, I., & Brzakovic, M. (2019). Importance of information in crisis management: Statistical analysis. *Industija, 47*(3).

Woo, R. (2015). Crisis leadership: Guiding the organization through uncertainty and chaos. *Deloitte & Touche LLP*.

About the Contributors

Dr. Michael Bailey is a former K-12 special education teacher, school district administrator, and currently the Director of Accessibility Services for Saint Leo University. His areas of expertise include educational policy, programming for students with disabilities, and developing instructional systems to support diverse learners. Michael holds master's degrees in the areas of Special Education and Educational Leadership and a doctorate in Educational Leadership from the University of South Florida.

Dr. Melinda Carver earned her PhD in Literacy Curriculum and Instruction from Walden University and has additional cognates in Educational Leadership and Instructional Design. She worked in public and private K-12 schools for over twenty years as a classroom teacher, math specialist, reading specialist, reading coach, and director. She is currently the Director of Program Approval and the Reading Program Administrator at Saint Leo University where she has designed and taught reading, technology, and assessment courses in the Reading, Exceptional Student Education, Instructional Leadership, and Education Doctorate programs. Her research interests are in the areas of literacy, educational technology, and assessment.

Dr. Ed Dadez has worked in the field of College and University Student Affairs for the past thirty-nine years. He has worked at and has degrees from Virginia Commonwealth University, Ohio State University, Michigan State University, and Saint Leo University. He has also taught college courses at six universities. After eighteen years, he retired from his Vice President for Student Affairs and Campus Operations position at Saint Leo University in May 2018 and returned as faculty member in the graduate education department.

About the Contributors

Dr. Susan Kinsella is the current Dean of the College of Education and Social Services and Professor of Human Services at Saint Leo University. She has a PhD in Social Work from Fordham University, an MSW from Marywood University, and a BSW from Pennsylvania. She has over twenty-five years of teaching and administrative experience in higher education, having developed and taught in undergraduate and graduate programs in Human Services and Social Work. Her clinical expertise is in child welfare, where she practiced and administered a child welfare program in Pennsylvania. She has numerous publications in social service journals, which include such topics as child welfare worker competencies, university and community collaborations, building leadership capacity, service learning, and global and social entrepreneurships.

Dr. Jodi Lamb obtained her doctorate from the University of South Florida. She has over twenty-eight years of experience in medium and large public school districts in elementary, middle/high school, and district office. She served as a media specialist, coach, professional developer, assistant principal, and principal. Currently, she is an associate professor and serves as the associate director for graduate education at Saint Leo University.

Dr. Keya Mukherjee received her PhD from the University of South Florida in Curriculum and Instruction, with emphasis on Applied Linguistics and Instructional Technology and Instructional Design. She has a bachelor's and a master's degrees in English as well as master's degree in Applied Linguistics/ESL. Prior to her work with Saint Leo, she worked for many years teaching ESL students and conducted teacher training in the United States and internationally. She is currently the Program Administrator for the ESOL and Instructional Design programs at Saint Leo University, where she teaches courses on instructional design, teacher education courses related to ESOL, courses on diversity and multicultural education, and research methodology.

Dr. Georgina Rivera-Singletary is Associate Professor for Graduate Special Education at Saint Leo University. Her research interests include special populations, social justice, and policy for migrant students with disabilities and English learners. Dr. Rivera-Singletary has twenty years of K-12 public school experience with roles in school and district administration, migrant resource teacher, and high school foreign language classrooms.

Dr. Renee Sedlack earned a bachelor's degree in Elementary Education, a master's degree in Early Childhood Education, and a doctorate degree in

Educational Leadership and Policy Studies. She has worked forty-one years in public schools as a teacher, assistant principal, principal, and human resources director. Currently, Dr. Sedlack is Assistant Professor of Educational Leadership at Saint Leo University. Her research interest is in exploring innovative initiatives to close the achievement gap among underserved youth.

About the Editor

Dr. Fern Aefsky has over thirty years' experience as a teacher and administrator (principal, director, assistant superintendent, and superintendent) in public schools, has been an adjunct professor at various universities for twenty-four years, and is currently a Professor of Education and the Director of Graduate Studies in Education at Saint Leo University. Presentations, publications, and research focus on collaboratively working with interdisciplinary teams to increase student success through effective school leadership and proactive interventions for school stakeholders. Developing programs in higher education that meet the needs of school practitioners through collaborative work is a passion for professional growth and development.

Made in the USA
Monee, IL
27 October 2022